Advance Applause

"The work of Phil Callaway is a sparkling star."
—MAX LUCADO

"Reading Phil Callaway is like playing in Holy Sand. You're having so much fun, you don't realize how much has gone into your shoes and is now sticking to your life."
—CHRIS FABRY, author and host of
Moody Broadcasting Network's *Open Line*

"If laughter is good for the soul, then Phil Callaway's new book is doubly good, for not only does it administer a healthy dose of humor, but many beneficial spiritual lessons as well. If you wish to smile your way to contemplative thinking, read *Making Life Rich Without Any Money*."
—JANETTE OKE, bestselling author

"Once again, Phil Callaway has touched a nerve that hits all-too-close to home. This book is must-reading for anyone who wonders, 'When is enough enough?'"
—MIKE YORKEY, author and editor of
Focus on the Family magazine from 1986-1997

"Phil Callaway, one of the funniest and most profound humorists alive, has done it again! This time he reminds us of what's truly important. If the hustle-bustle of today's world has caused you to mix up your priorities hoping to get ahead, read this book. It'll make you laugh, make you think, maybe even make you cry. Most importantly, it will remind you (despite what your accountant says) how truly rich you already are."
—MARTHA BOLTON, Bob Hope's joke writer
and author of *Honey, the Carpet Needs Weeding*

"In his excellent style, Phil Callaway tells stories that will convince anybody that true wealth is deeper and simpler and nearer than we realize. If you've been running ragged on the money-making treadmill, here is relief . . . and proof that you may be richer than you realize."
—BRIAN PETERSON, editor, *New Man* magazine

"If the richest things in life are free, then Phil Callaway has a corner on the free market. Without trumpeting itself as such, this book is nourishment for the soul. It doesn't beat us over the head for our bad choices as much as it provides us with a longing for good ones. This book is a pleasant journey, fun to read and meat for the soul."
—JOHN FISCHER, author of *What on Earth Are We Doing?*

"With charming humor and gripping stories, Phil helps us take inventory of the things that matter most—both now and long after we've left this planet."

—TIM WILDMON, cohost of *Today's Issues,* and
vice president of the American Family Association

"This book is a winner. From its heartwarming stories to its crystal-clear message of simplicity, *Making Life Rich Without Any Money* will leave you challenged, changed, and chuckling. Don't just buy a copy of this book. Buy a dozen for your friends and family—and try to get a discount!"

—JOEL A. FREEMAN, author and chaplain of the
NBA Washington Wizards

"It is impossible to read this book without being changed. Changed in our demands. Our expectations. And our level of contentment. If you struggle to balance the stuff of earth with the demands of heaven, or if you long for a lightning bolt of joy, this is just the ticket."

—SIGMUND BROWER, author of *Double Helix*

"In the middle of a very busy day, I began to skim this book. I was soon lost in laughter and wistful envy, then, encouraged that I can get off the treadmill of 'success' and start enjoying real wealth. If you have ever wished for a more simple, more fulfilling life, read this book."

—KEN DAVIS, motivational speaker and author

"Phil Callaway is absolutely incapable of writing a dull sentence. When he sets his pen to humor, the pages dance with laughter. When he undertakes a more serious topic the text shimmers with insight and wisdom—though humor is always around the corner! Here he offers fresh suggestions on finding the TRUE riches of life. Rewards that dwarf anything involving dollars, stocks, or bonds."

—PAUL L. MAIER, author of *Josephus* and
A Skeleton in God's Closet

Making Life Rich Without Any Money

PHIL CALLAWAY

HARVEST HOUSE PUBLISHERS
Eugene, Oregon 97402

Cover by Design Point, Salem, Oregon

MAKING LIFE RICH WITHOUT
ANY MONEY
Copyright © 1998 by Phil Callaway
Published by Harvest House Publishers
Eugene, Oregon 97402

Library of Congress Cataloging-in-Publication Data
Callaway, Phil, 1961–
  Making life rich without any money / Phil Callaway
     p.   cm.
  Includes bibliographical references.
  ISBN 1-56507-899-3
    1. Success—Religious aspects—Christianity.
2. Christian life—Humor. 3. Callaway, Phil, 1961–
I. Title.
BV4598.3.C35   1998
248.4—dc21   98-15495
                                                        CIP

Printed in the United States of America.

02 03 /BC/ 10 9 8 7 6 5 4

For Dave, Dan, Tim, and Ruth.
From your rich little brother.

Contents

Contents

Acknowledgments

My BEST FRIEND, RAMONA. A TRULY RICH MAN IS ONE whose wife runs into his arms when his hands are empty. Your love, your faithfulness, and your offspring have made me a wealthy man. Thanks for allowing me to tell a difficult chapter in our story.

The hundreds who answered my question, "What has made your life rich?" Your much-appreciated insights on the lifestyles of the rich and not-so-famous were an inspiration. I wanted to pay you. Until I remembered the title of this book.

Max Lucado, Gloria Gaither, Michael Card, Elisabeth Elliot, Steve Green, Twila Paris, Chris Fabry, Josh McDowell, Mike Yorkey, Luis Palau, Larry Crabb, and Tony Campolo. For wonderful answers to my questions. For enriching my life with your work.

Carolyn McCready, a first-rate encourager; Terry Glaspey, a top-notch editor; and Bill Jensen, a pretty good golfer. Thanks, you three, for believing in this project from the start.

Vance Neudorf. For being an imperfect friend and allowing me the freedom to be the same. For walking with me through the shadows, celebrating with me in the light, and always pointing me higher. (P.S.—I'm still sorry about the lawnmower.)

Dad and Mom. They say misers aren't much fun to live with, but they make wonderful ancestors. Thankfully you weren't the former, but you are the latter. Thanks for giving me the best inheritance a guy could wish for.

And finally, to you, the reader. Thanks for entrusting me with your valuable time. I pledge not to waste it. May the message of this book change you, as it has changed me.

The Poor Little Rich Boy

"Money has never yet made anyone rich."
—Lucius Annaeus Seneca (circa 4 b.c.–a.d. 65)

Something marvelous took place on the Callaway family tree this past December: My parents celebrated their fifty-fifth wedding anniversary. As you know, a fifty-fifth anniversary is as rare these days as checkered zebras, so we blew up balloons, bought gifts, combed the grandkids' hair, and ordered pizza. When the festivities died down, we thought we'd better do something a little out of the ordinary, so we bought space in a city newspaper and placed these words beside a picture of the handsome couple:

Happy 55th Wedding Anniversary!
From the 5 of us
awaiting our inheritance.

Of course, those who know my parents laughed the loudest when they saw this. But not everyone joined them. When my older brother (a Baptist minister) delivered the ad to the paper, the lady in charge of the classifieds took a long look at it, exhaled slowly, then asked quite seriously, "You sure you wanna say this? Won't it start a family feud or something?"

11

She had a good point. After all, baby boomers stand to inherit seven trillion dollars over the next 20 years.[1] But we Callaway kids won't have much to fight over. You see, our parents spent their entire lives below what the government calls "the poverty line." When Mom and Dad pass through heaven's gates they will leave behind a few sticks of furniture, an antique clock, and a car that sometimes runs.

I wasn't always thankful for this.

As a five-year-old, I sat on the edge of the bathtub, two pennies in hand, and discovered to my surprise that by simply holding the coins in front of a mirror I could double my assets. *What would it be like to make money this quickly?* I wondered, before praying out loud, "God, please make me rich."

But God didn't seem to hear.

In those days, my father's monthly income was 230 dollars—hardly enough to buy sugar for my cereal. It's safe to say that the buck stopped before it got to our house. As a result, we had no television. No skateboards. No insurance. In fact, we couldn't even afford a phone. One night I overheard Dad say to Mom, "Honey, we have enough money to last us the rest of our lives. Unless we live past Thursday!"

Thursday came and went and the years slipped by. Then, ever so slowly, it began to dawn on me that my prayer was being answered. Not in the way I hoped it would be. But in a far better way. You see, at the age of 14, I still hadn't smelled the inside of a new car, savored a Big Mac, or slipped on a brand-new pair of jeans. But I had a backyard to run in, friends to play with, parents who loved me, and the rock-solid belief that God loved me too.

Through the years I have watched my fellow North Americans pursue wealth in all the wrong places. Just this morning I did a quick search on the Internet and discovered almost 37,000 web sites on how to get rich quick.

I could not find one on "making life rich."

Yet, when it comes right down to it, that's what we're all looking for, isn't it? Our television promises that a newer car, a colder drink, or a cuter wife will be just the ticket. The billboards assure us that a step up the ladder, a plane ride to somewhere exotic, or a worry-free journey to retirement will make our lives richer. But deep down, we know it's a lie. Still, millions of us spend our lives pursuing what we don't have . . . to the neglect of what we really need. And what is it that we really need? What is it that we're looking for?

In my quest to answer these questions, I began to ask people—young and old, rich and poor, famous and infamous— what has made their lives rich. Their answers surprised me. And formed the backbone of what you are about to read.

As a young boy in dilapidated jeans, sitting on the edge of the tub, I thought I knew what would make me rich. As a middle-aged man, I'm beginning to discover that truly rich people, whether they know it or not, share six characteristics.

I can't wait to tell you what they are.

Part I

RICH PEOPLE KNOW THE SPEED LIMIT

Most of us, if given enough time to think it over, know what makes our lives rich. We know what brings us joy, what glues a permanent smile to our faces. The trouble is, we're driving too fast to notice. We're too busy working overtime. Meeting deadlines. Running stoplights. And the things that make life rich are lost in the blur.

I don't know about you, but I'm so tired I get winded riding escalators. I'm tired of paying $14.95 for books that tell me how to save money. I'm tired of traffic jams, to-do lists, and microwave dinners. And most of all, I'm tired of trading the things that matter for the things that don't . . . all because I'm moving at the speed of stress.

But how do we slow down without pulling out of the race?

How do we jump off the roller coaster without getting flattened?

Three years ago, something happened that forced me to pull out of the fast lane. And look around for the answers.

CHAPTER ONE

Slowing Down in a Speeded-Up World

"The trouble with being in the rat race is that even if you're win, you're still a rat."

—LILY TOMLIN

NOT FAR FROM OUR HOME A TINY POND RESTS, shaded by elder bushes and nourished by underground streams. At night I occasionally stroll past the pond, watching ducks practice their runway approaches amid the choruses of redwing blackbirds and the croaking of mud-drenched frogs. But tonight all is quiet. Tonight a hot, dry summer has taken its toll and there is no blackbird chorus. No croaking frogs. No splash landings.

The pond, you see, is drying up.

Three years ago right now I felt like that pond. Flat on my back, I was finished. Kaput. Burned-out.

Five years on a treadmill had taken its toll. Five years of chasing dreams, but finding little sleep. Of pursuing success, but finding little peace. Midnights writing books had been tacked onto 50-hour workweeks, weekend speaking engagements, and the nurturing of a growing family. Worst of all, the circumstances I will tell you about in chapter 9 had set my life on edge. Each day began at seven, and ended about 19 hours later, if insomnia allowed me to sleep.

I was climbing the ladder with my nose to the grindstone, my shoulder to the wheel, and my eye on the ball. But like a clumsy juggler, I watched helplessly as things began to hit the ground. Like the dried-up pond, I listened hopelessly for the blackbird's song, but none came.

I knew, as you do, that we live in a speeded-up world. People headed for Europe used to spend months relaxing on ocean liners. Breathing deeply of the salt air. Savoring novels and visiting friends. Now we can make the same trip in less than a day, and when we get there, we're itching to be first off the plane. Last year the average full-time employee worked 138 hours more than the average worker did 20 years ago.

Is the world a better place than it was in the days of the ocean liner?

While trying to program my VCR recently, I thought to myself: *Can you believe how much technology is out there that we never asked for?* I mean, who said we need split-screen televisions, freeze-frame remotes, and fancy delay features on our dishwashers? Who said we need clocks that make coffee, satellites to find our car keys, and cameras that talk? I love bread makers and microwaves, but what I'd like more than anything right now is to lie down for a full hour without the phone ringing. I've been trying to program my car radio since 1986. I've been reading instruction manuals since before that. This is the Aspirin Age and my head is pounding. If I had the time, I'd sit down and write a letter:

> *Dear Guys Who Come Up with More Stuff:*
>
> Please stop. We're fine. We have enough RAM in our computers and enough room in our trunks. Our jets go fast enough now. Please work on an invention that slows us down. That brings families together. That cures diseases. I'm still trying to figure out my e-mail.

But the stuff keeps coming. This week I found out that you can now buy a gas-powered blender to use in the backyard. How times have changed since Daniel Boone said, "All you need for happiness is a good gun, a good horse, and a good wife."

The experts tell us that each day in America:

- 108,000 people move to a different home and 18,000 to a different state.
- 45,000 new vehicles are purchased.
- 87,000 vehicles are smashed.
- 11 billion e-mails are downloaded.
- 20,000 people write letters to the president.
- 75 acres of pizza are eaten, as well as 53 million hot dogs and 3 million gallons of ice cream. (Then we jog 17 million miles to burn off all those calories.)[2]

The increasing speed at which we live is costing us what we value most. We are crowding each day with more work than it can profitably hold, and it's costing us the undisturbed enjoyment of friends. And sometimes it's costing us our health.

Kenneth Greenspan of New York's Presbyterian Hospital claims that stress now contributes to 90 percent of all diseases.[3] Incredibly, anxiety-reduction may now be the largest single business in the Western world.

In a recent study of 11,500 ministers, three out of four reported severe stress causing "anguish, worry, bewilderment, anger, depression, fear, and alienation."

I meet people all the time who feel this way. Who feel like I did three years ago. For them the birds have stopped singing. The pond has dried up. *When will the streams flow again?* they wonder. *How do we find peace in a noisy culture?* they ask.

The other night as spring touched down, I took a walk with my nine-year-old daughter, Rachael. Hand in hand we followed a cattle path past blossoming violets and dandelions until the ground fell abruptly away to reveal our favorite pond.

Sure enough, the songbirds were back.

Sure enough, the underground streams were flowing once again.

As we tossed small stones into the water, I thought of my own long winter. And the things that had helped me most.

CHAPTER TWO

Speechless in Seattle

"Here's to our town—a place where people spend money they haven't earned to buy things they don't need to impress people they don't like."

—LEWIS C. HENRY

HE SITS IN A TINY OFFICE, WIPING SWEAT FROM his brow. A smile crosses his face as he picks up the phone. The place is New Delhi, India. The year is 1958. "I would like to place an order," he says into the receiver. "I would like 10,000 fountain pen caps." At the other end of the line, surprise is registered by silence. Then, "We'll be glad to fill your order, sir, but . . . well, what do you plan to do with 10,000 fountain pen caps?"

"Here in India," the young entrepreneur explains, "one who has a pen in his shirt pocket is considered both wealthy and intelligent. I will sell only the tops of the pens. It makes no difference if they can write."

Within two days of arriving in New Delhi, every single fountain pen cap has been sold. And once again the man with the smile on his face enters his tiny office and picks up the phone.

The best stories are those in which we see ourselves, and if we're honest, we won't have to look far in this one. Too many of us spend a lifetime lining our pockets with surface stuff that makes us seem successful, but down below, down where it really counts, we are as empty as a New Delhi pen cap.

Flat on my back, burned-out and desperate, I began to take an honest look at my life. What was pushing me to travel so fast? To work so hard? I had to admit it: It was the drive to acquire surface stuff. To give my family the things I never had. A secure future. An exotic vacation. And jeans without patches.

One morning the phone rang. It was the president of a successful California corporation asking me to consider a prestigious position in his firm. The starting salary? Three times what I was making at the time.

It didn't take long for a smile to cross my face. "Wouldn't it be nice to have a little extra money?" I told my wife, Ramona. "You could use a new wardrobe and I'd love to buy some of the things I've always wanted. A car that won't quit. A house that won't leak. And the kids will love it, too. We'll be close to Disneyland."

"Once I get some new clothes, I'd love to do some traveling," said Ramona, nodding her head. "Maybe visit some relatives."

I wasn't quite sure about the relatives part, but two weeks later we were on our way to California for a formal interview.

Oak boardrooms and exquisite offices have always intimidated me, but this time I felt right at home. This was where I belonged. My sights were set on a bigger house. A newer car. Security. Success. All I had to do was squeeze the trigger.

During the interview, I was intrigued by all that the job offered. A chance to better myself. To work with people. A chance to travel. "How many days a month will I be on the road?" I asked.

There was an uncomfortable silence.

The president looked at me as if he didn't understand the question. Finally he said, "The question isn't how much you'll be gone, Phil. It's how much you'll be home. And it won't be much."

Ramona was nudging me under the table, a wrinkled expression on her face. And later that day on the flight home she expressed her concern. "You have a young family, Phil . . . we'd really like to see you occasionally. . . . Life is lived in chapters. We need you to play a leading role in this one. Besides, we're Christians . . . we need to spend more time praying about this."

But during our layover in Seattle, I renewed my determination to take the job. As I walked to a nearby restroom, I practiced my acceptance speech. The offer was too good to refuse. I would call California from home.

Entering a tiny stall, I latched the door behind me. Suddenly the place began to shake. Lights flickered. Doors rattled. Walls shook. For the first time in my life, I was in an earthquake. Now I don't know if you've thought much about dying, or if you've thought about *where* you would most like to die, but if you're anything like me, your list does not include an airport washroom.

During the next few seconds, brief memories flashed before me: The miraculous birth of our first child. Faces of friends and family. My wife. My kids. There was not one image of a car, a home, or a bulging bank account.

As the rattling stopped, a man in the cubicle next to me said loudly, "Did I do that?"

I was speechless.

Unlatching the door, I ran quickly from the room, hoping to hold my wife before being encased in rubble. *I'll kiss her,* I thought, *and let her feel the earth move one last time!*

Later we learned that the quake had registered 5.0 on Mr. Richter's scale. Believe me, it registered much higher on mine.

On the flight home, I scribbled for the first time ever my personal mission statement:

> I will consider myself a success when I am walking close to Jesus every day. When I am building a strong marriage, loving my kids, and performing meaningful work.

"I'll call California," I told Ramona, taking her hand. And she knew from the smile on my face what I planned to say.

———•———

Looking back on those days, I can see that my journey on the road to recovery started with a simple statement scribbled on an airline napkin. You see, 100 years from now, no one will remember what kind of house I lived in, what model car I drove, or the size of my bank account. One hundred years from now, no one will remember how many bestsellers I wrote, or how many pens lined my pocket.

But the world may be a better place because I slowed down enough to listen to God's voice. Because I was important in the eyes of a child. Because I learned to be content with the things I did not have.

For in the end, the things that matter most are not really things, after all.

CHAPTER THREE

A Parachute and a Promise

"When you have accomplished your daily task, go to sleep in peace; God is awake."

—Victor Hugo (1802–1885)

Road signs, they say, are designed to steer us safely in the right direction. Some (like the sort police officers point out when it's too late) seem designed only to frustrate us. But occasionally a sign pops up which brings a smile to my face.

On one of the highest mountains in the Colorado Rockies is such a sign. It simply says: "Hill." On the Alaska Highway is another: "Choose your rut carefully. You'll be in it for the next 200 miles."

Three years ago the rut I'd carved out for so long grew too deep and my engine ground to a halt. An obsession with trying to get ahead had gotten me nowhere but behind. But what could I do? A doctor advised me to take six months off. But how could I? I had a growing family and a shrinking bank account. Besides, none of us can insulate ourselves from stress. It is part of life.

Looking back now, I realize that I needed to hear of a better way. Over time, three practical truths would begin to get through to me, helping me steer clear of the rut I had traveled in for so long.

1. Laughter is a tranquilizer with no side effects.

Serious students of laughter tell us that the average toddler laughs about 200 times a day. But by the time the average toddler becomes an average adult, he registers only six laughs a day. Tell me, where did we lose 194 laughs? I have a theory. I think we start losing them when we enter first grade. I think they begin to vanish when our teacher singles us out and says in a stern voice, "Would you stand and tell us what is so funny?"

By the time we're out of school, we have jobs to think about. We have debts to pay, appointments to keep, and children to diaper.

Just before dinner one night, the phone rang. My daughter, Rachael, who was five, answered: "Now I lay me down to sleep..." Then, clapping her hand over her mouth, she said, "Whoops!"

I'm ashamed to say that I sat nearby, more concerned about who was on the other end of the line than the hilarity of the moment. After dinner, Jeffrey, our youngest, said to me, "Dad, you don't laugh so good." Here I was, a humor writer, but the laughter was gone. That night, after tucking in the kids, I pulled out some old Pink Panther movies and began practicing my laugh. Then I determined to spend more time with my kids, studying their laughter and seeing if it was contagious.

Gloria Gaither says that children laugh so much because they are "so fresh from God." Perhaps she's right. Jeffrey, our youngest, loves nothing more than a good laugh. If given the chance, this little guy will laugh at the same joke 200 times in a row. He's a stand-up comedian's dream. Often he will start to tell us a joke, but he seldom finishes. Halfway through he is laughing so hard that his brother has to finish it for him. And Jeffrey sits nearby, hyperventilating.

Knowing that it is a proven fact that laughter reduces stress, a good friend came to visit one day and handed me a list of proverbs. The list was collected by a first-grade teacher with a great sense of humor. She had given her students the first part of an old proverb and asked them to fill in the rest. The hilarious results are still pinned to my bulletin board as a reminder not to miss out on the laughter of children.

Old proverbs revisited by the young
Better to be safe than . . . punch a fifth grader.
Strike while the . . . bug is close.
Don't bite the hand that . . . looks dirty.
Children should be seen and not . . . spanked.
Happy the bride who . . . gets all the presents.
There is none so blind as . . . Helen Keller.
Where there's smoke there's . . . pollution.
A penny saved is . . . not much.
There is no fool like . . . Uncle Eddie.

In the darkest of times, I have discovered that laughter tends to revolutionize my perspective. Like the sun, laughter can drive winter from the human face. I have watched it happen so often. Laughter adds richness and texture to our lives. It adds bright color to ordinary days. Laughter is a gift, but it is also a choice, a discipline, and an art. G. K. Chesterton said, "Angels can fly because they take themselves lightly." The same is true of people.

2. There's a heavy penalty for resisting a rest.

A man sent his psychiatrist a postcard. It said, "Am having a great time on vacation. Wish you were here to tell me why."

Three years ago I realized I had not taken a two-week vacation in ten years, and I didn't need a psychiatrist to tell me I was in trouble. Here I was an author, but I couldn't spell *rest*. In trying to save time, I'd forgotten how to spend it. Where had I learned my work ethic? It certainly wasn't from studying the life of Jesus. Never does the Bible give us any evidence to suggest that He labored in an occupation to the point of constant emotional exhaustion. No one in history accomplished more, yet He did so without acquiring an ulcer. And several times the Bible tells us that He took a break.

In the midst of the darkest chapter of my life, I began to follow Jesus' example. The first thing I did was to quit going to work before everyone else. Then I determined to take a break from the daily newspaper. Then came exercising in our local aquatic center and enjoying some hobbies I'd always been too busy for. On Saturdays I painted our shed, and at night I never missed an opportunity to read to the kids.

While painting the shed one Saturday, I discovered an old wooden bird feeder. The years had peeled its paint back, leaving long, ugly scars. I spent an hour or two scraping and repainting, then filled the feeder with birdseed, hung it near the shed, and watched to see who would take the bait.

Sure enough, an ordinary sparrow descended from the trees, steadied itself on the edge of the feeder and, with me watching, pecked contentedly away at the tiny seeds. Before long it flew up into a tree, turned its head to one side, and fell asleep.

Above, the sky was furrowed with threatening bands of gray, yet the sparrow rocked itself gently to sleep. Without a care for tomorrow's lodging. Without a thought of the location of its next meal. A tiny sparrow, clinging calmly to a twig. And leaving the rest up to God.

3. There's only one place to find the missing peace.

Someone told me a story the other day. A story that made me laugh, then made me think. It seems that a young man who had wanted to skydive all his life finally got the chance. Of course, if you're skydiving, it's a good idea to take a lesson or two. So he did. During the final lesson, his wise instructor told him what to do. "First, jump when you are told. Second, count to ten and pull the rip cord. Third, in the very unlikely event that it doesn't work, pull the second chute open. And fourth, when you get down, a truck will take you back to the airport."

Butterflies of anticipation churned within him as the plane ascended to the proper height. When the time was right, the young man jumped, counted to ten, and pulled the rip cord.

Nothing.

So he pulled the second cord. It, too, failed.

"Oh sure," he muttered out loud, "I'll bet the truck won't even be there when I get down."

Have you ever felt like that skydiver? I have. When I was in sixth grade, I lived in terror. Specifically, I feared that my parents would be killed in a car accident. Whenever they went away, I lived in misery. Whenever they were gone, I waited for a stern-faced adult to enter the room and break the tragic news of their demise. I knew that no one would be there to pick me up.

One day while my parents were away, I left our school yard at recess and ran home to throw myself in tears on their bed. Looking up, I saw a tiny picture of a peaceful forest scene. The picture had been placed there before I was born. As a toddler I had taken afternoon naps below that picture. When I was five I had gazed up at it for comfort during the occasional spanking. But not until the age of six did I notice that the picture highlighted these words:

> Thou wilt keep him in perfect peace, whose mind is stayed on Thee: because he trusteth in Thee. Trust in the LORD forever, for in God the LORD, we have an everlasting Rock (Isaiah 26:3,4).

Those were some of the first words I ever read. But I'm just starting to understand them. Every time I strap myself into an airplane, every time I lie awake wondering about tomorrow, I must practice that trust.

The world around us knows little of perfect peace. One authority says that in more than 3500 years of recorded civilization, 8000 peace treaties were broken, and only 286 of those years were spent without war taking place somewhere.[4] What's true for the planet is true for its people. We rarely experience peace. We live anxious lives. We worry. We give in to fear.

Yet tucked away in that forest scene is the key to finding the missing peace we all long for. When an uncertain future looms ahead, God says, "Lift your eyes a little higher." When unpleasant circumstances close in, God says, "Trust Me. I will not let you down."

Three years ago, after an evening of playing with the kids, I took a walk by myself. To my right, a busy highway dotted with road signs stretched on ahead. To my left, sun-drenched wheat fields rolled across the prairies and swelled against the mountains. As cars drove by in a steady stream of traffic, I finally released the things I had held so tightly for so long. "God," I prayed out loud, "I want to trust You completely for my finances, my family, and my future. You are big enough to handle them all."

I'd like to say it's been a smooth ride ever since. But it hasn't. There are still times when I'm anxious. Times when I'm stressed. Times when I find myself in the same old rut. That's when I need to be reminded of a parachute and a promise. The parachute reminds me that we live in stressful times. But the promise tucked away in a tiny picture is a reminder that we need not worry. Someone will be there to catch us. Every time.

CHAPTER FOUR

The Riches of Simplicity

"It is better to live rich than to die rich."
—SAMUEL JOHNSON (1709–1784)

WE LIVE IN A SMALL TOWN, POPULATION 3417 (including pets). No traffic lights. No malls. No frills. You sneeze while driving past and you'll miss us every time. We've had opportunity to live elsewhere, but this is the suit that fits us best for now.

Some of my best friends are city folk. They love the bustle. The noises. The choices. They thrive on cell phones. On lunch meetings. On car-pool lanes.

Not me. Many weekends you'll find me in the city, but when I point my car toward home it's like someone loosened my tie. I enjoy living on a street that's so quiet you can sit on your back porch and *listen* to the sun set. I enjoy getting up each day knowing that a ten-minute walk to work will clear my sinuses, and that if I left my car lights on the night before, a neighbor probably went out in his slippers and shut them off.

In a recent cover story, "Why Americans Are Fleeing to Small Towns," *Time* magazine pointed out that in the 1990s two million more Americans moved from cities to rural areas than migrated the other way. Jim Wiley of Wilmington, Ohio, was one. In the article he says, "Living in Los Angeles, my vision became blurred and twisted. I was spoiled. I had secretaries doing everything for me. All I did was talk on the phone and sit in traffic. In L.A. I endured 15 solid years of sunshine. All those rays every day—they aggravated me."

Living in a small town can blur your vision too. You see, it's easier here to slow down to an unhealthy crawl. To sit on the porch each evening watching the bug-zapper and forgetting that there's a world out there that could use my help. That's when I need to remember that slowing down in a speeded-up world does not mean taking a permanent exit to Easy Street. God does not call us to rest seven days a week with our head in the sand. He calls us to make an impact wherever we are. But in order to do that, it's important to slow down and focus on the things that matter most. Remember His words, "Be still, and know that I am God" (Psalm 46:10), and ". . . in quietness and trust is your strength" (Isaiah 30:15).

The other day I asked my 11-year-old son, Stephen, "If you had your life to live over again, what would you do differently?" Before he knew I was kidding, he answered, "Eat more candy."

I laughed at first, but the more I thought about his words, the more I realized the wisdom in them.

You see, I have yet to hear someone in an old folks' home say, "I wish I would have spent more time with my computer," or, "I wish I would have worried more and laughed less." But I know too many who are spending the last half of a busy life regretting the first half.

A frenzied friend of mine has this on his desk: "We the willing, led by the unknowing, are doing the impossible for the ungrateful. We have done so much for so long with so little we are now qualified to do anything with nothing."

Late in life, an anonymous friar in a Nebraska monastery wrote the following words. I sent them to my friend. He's still trying to get up enough nerve to show them to his boss.

> If I had my life to live over again, I'd try to make more mistakes next time.
> I would relax, I would limber up, I would be sillier than I have been on this trip.
> I know of very few things I would take seriously.
> I would take more trips. I would be crazier.
> I would climb more mountains, swim more rivers, and watch more sunsets.
> I would do more walking and looking.
> I would eat more ice cream and less beans.
> I would have more actual troubles, and fewer imaginary ones.
> You see, I'm one of those people who lives life prophylactically and sensibly hour after hour, day after day. Oh, I've had my moments, and if I had to do it over again, I'd have more of them.
> In fact, I'd try to have nothing else, just moments, one after another, instead of living so many years ahead each day. I've been one of those people who never goes

anywhere without a thermometer, a hot-water bottle,
  a gargle, a raincoat, aspirin, and a parachute.
If I had it to do all over again, I would go places, do
  things, and travel lighter than I have.
If I had my life to live over, I would start barefooted
  earlier in the spring and stay that way later in the fall.
I would play hookey more.
I wouldn't make such good grades, except by accident.
I would ride on more merry-go-rounds.
I'd pick more daisies.

Of course, I'm not for playing hookey (believe me, my kids know this), but sometimes I wonder where I got the notion that God is only pleased with my work. In the same way that I love to watch my children chase one another down a sandy beach, so God is pleased when we go barefoot. In the same way that I cheer when my daughter sinks a basketball (yes, this has happened), so God is pleased when we play.

When I was a boy, I heard people say that it's better to burn out than to rust out, and I found myself wondering if there wasn't a better alternative. Years later I've noticed that some of those very same people are the most miserable humans I know. In chasing dreams they missed waking up to the simple joys around them. In climbing a ladder they failed to see that it was leaning against a crumbling wall.

I haven't arrived yet. I'm still learning to juggle a busy schedule while enjoying the simple gifts God gives. I'm still learning that there is freedom in slowing down. That there are riches in simplicity. And most of all, I'm learning that there is freedom in following the example of Jesus. After all, He carried the weight of the world on His shoulders, but slept soundly in the bottom of a storm-tossed boat. After all, He changed the course of history and still had time to hold little children on His lap.

Will you determine with me to forget keeping up with the Joneses? To stop chasing things we can't cram in our coffins?

Whether you find yourself in the car-pool lane or out watching the bug-zapper, it can make all the difference.

31 Ways to Simplify Your Life

1. Try everything offered by supermarket food demonstrators.
2. Reread a favorite book.
3. If possible, have a pet.
4. Take your child for a walk (if you don't have a child, borrow one from a friend).
5. Refrain from envy. Genuinely compliment those who have more than you.
6. Make Sunday a day of rest. Start by leaving your watch off (especially during the sermon).
7. Learn to say no politely and quickly.
8. Learn more about the stars. Then lie on your back and find them.
9. Live by the calendar, not the stopwatch.
10. Each day when you wake up, let your first activity be prayer.
11. Wave at children on school buses.
12. Plan some leisure time each day.
13. Buy a bird feeder and hang it outside your window.
14. Learn to enjoy food. Take longer to eat it.

15. Don't major on minor issues.
16. Attend your child's recitals and plays. Compliment the teacher.
17. Don't give your kids the best of everything. Give them your best.
18. Never miss a chance to read a child a story.
19. When you're alone in the car, sing loudly. Don't forget to roll up the windows!
20. As often as you can, give thanks.
21. Avoid negative or overly competitive people.
22. Wear a wild T-shirt under your suit occasionally.
23. Change into casual clothes when you get home from work.
24. When you can, buy secondhand.
25. Remember, God doesn't have a watch.
26. As soon as you can, pay your debts.
27. Find a good reason to laugh today.
28. Forget the Joneses.
29. Give something away.
30. Meditate on Matthew chapter 6.
31. Observe the speed limit.

CHAPTER FIVE

Lifestyles of the Rich and Not-So-Famous

"No man can tell whether he is rich or poor by turning to his wallet. It is the heart that makes a man rich."

—Henry Ward Beecher (1813–1887)

Some time ago I began asking people on airplanes, in checkout lines, and on e-mail one simple question: "What has made your life rich?" One of them turned on me rather abruptly and said, "When people like you leave me alone!"

Thankfully, most found the question a little more interesting, though, and a few hundred were good enough to respond. They ranged from bestselling authors to concert pianists to real-estate agents. But no matter what their occupation, many share one thing in common. They are realizing that those who slow down enough to enjoy the simple gifts God gives enrich their lives. Here is a small sampling. I hope you'll enjoy these responses as much as I have.

———•———

"We picked up an old dog at the pound last year and named him George. His previous owner abused him and he limps a bit, but when I come home from work, George somehow finds a way to wag just about everything. He doesn't seem to care how successful I was at the office, or how many sales I made that day. He just cares that I'm home. I grew up with an abusive father, and whenever George greets me at the door, I'm reminded that though we both carry scars from the past, we can do something about our outlook on the future. George's limp reminds me of the need for gentleness in my life. An old dog is teaching me new tricks . . . and making my life rich."[5]

———•———

"Money hasn't made my life rich (although I wouldn't mind trying it out for a while), but knowing Christ has. I am profoundly enriched to know that the Creator of the universe stoops to care about me. He cares when I have a bad day or a bad week or a bad haircut. As the years go by, our budget seems to be shrinking. This month my husband lost his job. Yet God has always taken care of us and I know that will never change."

———•———

"One thing that has made my life rich without costing anything is a library card. I've trudged through the sewers of France, gone shrimping off the coast of South Carolina, been in the inner chambers of the White House—all through reading great books. Books have opened a world outside my own. Books have shown me there's more to life than my little existence. Books have broadened my horizons, challenged me to take risks, and best of all, have shown me the true path to God, through His Son Jesus Christ."

———•———

"I recently rediscovered the Sabbath. Now, instead of shopping, fixing the car, or cleaning the house, our family attends an early church service then spends the day together. We have hiked into the Rocky Mountains singing at the top of our lungs. We have serenaded the patrons of old folks' homes. And we have sat under pine trees reading the classics together. Always we are better prepared for Monday because of Sunday."

———•———

"When my husband and I were engaged, the prospect of moving into a house was daunting because all of our possessions wouldn't even fill a room. We had very little money, so purchasing furniture was out of the question. But members of my church gave us a kitchen table with chairs and two big, comfortable living-room chairs. A landlady gave us a bed and a washer. My mom bought new mattresses for the bed and a couch for the living room. Friends donated shelves, an end table, and kitchen accessories. At four separate bridal showers and the wedding, relatives and friends heaped gifts on us. We have been married now for almost eight years and when we look around our home we can recall the names of friends and family who gave certain gifts. If we had been financially well-off our decor would have been more stylish, but the rooms would not have been filled with the joy of hundreds of friends. Money creates independence, but it can rob us of sharing our needs with others and expressing our joy and thanksgiving at their generosity."

———

"I am a homemaker with two small children and one husband. In the last year I have learned to look positively on the smallest tasks. When I unload the dishwasher, I think of those who will eat off the forks. When I unload the dryer, I sometimes hug the warm clothes, and pray for those who will wear them."

———

"I grew up a missionary kid in Africa. I could tell it was difficult for my parents to make ends meet some months, but we never went without that I can recall. Sure, we never had steak at home, but we had vacations, fishing trips, and bicycles. We even got to see the world. It sounds funny, but to this day if given the choice, I'll take a hamburger over a steak anytime."

———

"My father taught me how to fish when I was very young. The fun of catching a big one has never left me, but I'm equally excited to watch my kids or one of their friends reel one in. My dad died this past year and my son graduated from high school. For his graduation present we spent a week together fishing in Minnesota. The last night, when we were bringing in the boat, the weather was perfect and the scenery was beautiful. I was pretty emotional, knowing he was on his way to university and this may never happen again. But I also knew that just like me, he would never forget fishing with his dad."

Part II

RICH PEOPLE
HIT CURVEBALLS

The richest people I know are not those who have lived the easiest life or watched the sun rise into a blue sky every morning. They don't always pick up the phone to good news, or respond with grace to every crisis. But they are learning how to stand in the batter's box and take a swing when life throws them a curveball. They are learning where to turn when the road starts to wind unexpectedly. They know that those who trust, triumph; that those who laugh, last; that those who weather the storm do so because their roots reach deep into the soil and hang onto the rock.

When I think of rich people, I think of the people you are about to meet.

CHAPTER SIX

While They Were Sleeping

"If you don't learn to laugh at trouble, you won't have anything to laugh at when you're old."

—ED HOWE (1853–1937)

I WISH YOU COULD MEET JIM AND JEAN SOUTH-worth. They're my kind of people. No one understands better than the Southworths that when things go wrong, it is our attitude that makes all the difference.

About 5:30 one morning, Jim, Jean, and their three children were sound asleep inside their home on a peaceful residential street in Salem, Oregon. Their eldest son had just poured himself a drink of milk in the kitchen and headed back to bed for a few more hours of sleep. But outside the house, things were taking shape that would put a serious dent in the Southworths' plans.

On a nearby hillside, the Curly's Dairy man rolled his van to a stop for a routine delivery. But when he returned, his mouth dropped open in horror as his van took a turn for the worse. Down the hill it went, backwards and gathering speed. The van jumped a few curbs and took out a maple tree. It flattened some shrubs and toppled a picket fence. Finally, it leveled the Southworths' front porch and crashed to a halt in their darkened kitchen.

"It was like a bomb went off," recalls Jim, a dentist. When his wife, Jean, saw the mess, she did what any homemaker would do: She cried over a spilt milk truck. But when she saw the slogan on the van staring out at her from the ruins of her kitchen, the tears vanished. "Here Comes Curly," it said. And Jean started to laugh.

When the dust settled, Jim managed to talk Curly's out of three gallons of ice cream, though he said he would have preferred a year's worth of milk. Jean wasn't so sure she wanted Curly's delivering anything to her house ever again. After all, the front porch was totaled. The eating nook was toast. And the front door? Well . . . no one quite knew where it was.

"A few years ago when an earthquake hit," Jean told me, "Jim thought we'd been hit by a truck. That morning he thought we were having an earthquake."

Insurance covered the 15,000 dollars' damage, and Jim and Jean decided the time was right to do a little renovation. "Our remodeler said we saved on demolition costs," laughs Jean, "although they don't normally use Curly's for that. We're wondering about the poor driver. He's probably in therapy. We hear that Salem customers cower in mock terror at approaching dairy trucks."

When the renovations were complete, Jim and Jean decided to throw a party to celebrate the closing of an open house. First they convinced Curly's Dairy to park a truck out front. A handmade sign instructed the driver where to park: "Please park IN FRONT of the house not INSIDE the house. Thanks." In the flower beds, another sign read, "Danger. Runaway truck zone." Through the truck window a Curly's manager served up eight flavors of ice cream. And in the kitchen 67 guests gathered to browse through the accident photos.

"When we first heard the crash and saw the crumpled walls of our house that morning," says Jean, "we thought this was the end for all of us. But once we realized we'd only been smashed into by a delivery truck, we calmed down. Our entryway and kitchen nook were destroyed, but our kids were okay. That's what matters. Besides, what good would getting upset do?"

Did they consider a lawsuit? "Never," says Jean. "But we were surprised at the number of people who wanted us to. It was fun seeing our story on the front page of the newspaper, but we were left wondering why our reaction was considered so unusual as to be newsworthy at all. That's the way it's supposed to be, isn't it? After all, we're Christians. We're supposed to practice love and forgiveness."

At first, friends who saw the devastation didn't know what to say. But once they found out that the South-worths didn't mind talking about their adventure, they started calling. "Hey, I heard your house got creamed by a dairy truck!" said one. Another told Jean that if she had to get hit by a large vehicle, she hoped it would be an ice-cream truck, too.

Nowadays people in Salem call Jean "the ice-cream lady," but she doesn't mind. "Pulitzer prize winners know what the first line will be in their obituaries," she smiles.

"At my funeral I'm sure somebody will say something about the day we got creamed by a dairy truck."

For the Southworths, life is a looking glass. Frown into it and it will frown back at you. Laugh with it and you will find it a kindly companion.

Some may think the Southworths are a bit crazy, and Jim and Jean might agree. But I know from talking to them that after watching others worry most about the things that matter least, they made a decision to hold things loosely. To quietly commit everything they have to God. And to live their lives with thanksgiving.

"No matter what happens to us there's always something to be thankful for," says Jean. "In our case, God protected us. The Curly's truck could have easily come into our bedroom instead of the kitchen early that morning.

"Besides," she laughs, "my husband is a dentist. He's used to filling cavities."

CHAPTER SEVEN

How to Live with Empty Pockets

"My attitude determines whether grief causes a disease in me or a glorious and everlasting reward."

—S. I. McMillen

SOME WRITERS IMPRESS US WITH PULITZER prizes, with prestigious awards and plaques of honor. Others earn a far more permanent place in our hearts when their words are taped to our refrigerators.

I noticed recently that a friend's wife had fastened these words to her fridge:

Lord, if You can't make me thin, make my friends look fat.

I found myself wondering who wrote the words and, after a little digging, I was finally able to uncover the fascinating answer.

51

She was only nine when her father died, leaving her and her mother flat broke. Their only option for survival was to move to an economically depressed neighborhood to live with the in-laws—a family of ten. Working as a copy girl at a local newspaper, she earned enough money to attend college where she hoped to pursue her dream—the dream of becoming a writer. But as her grades plummeted, the dream fell apart, and a guidance counselor advised her not to ever consider a career in writing.

Somehow she managed to laugh off the advice, though, and finally was able to land a job writing the obituaries in a local newspaper. Her mother told her that the only thing she accomplished in those days was getting the people to die in alphabetical order. But still she pressed on.

At the age of 20, she was diagnosed with a kidney disorder which two of her children would later inherit.

Determined to rise above it all, she began writing humorous articles about life as a stay-at-home mom. The articles caught on. The phone started ringing. And before long, she was writing one of the most widely syndicated columns of all time, and brightening the lives of millions through humor books like *It's Always Greener Over the Septic Tank*, and *When You Look Like Your Passport Photo, It's Time to Go Home*.

When asked to write a book about children with cancer, she said no. How could one find humor in such a situation? But after talking with children at a special camp for kids with cancer, she knew she had to. One day she asked one of the children, "What would you want if you had three wishes?"

His words became the title of her book: "I want to grow hair, I want to grow up, I want to go to Boise."

The book changed her life.

As she described it, "Things that were important before don't seem worth worrying about now. I'm more of a one day at a time person. I think about the three-year-old boy who threw his arms around me and said, 'You know what? I'm going to the circus!' The counselor corrected him, saying they were going swimming. Without missing a beat the kid said, 'You know what? I'm going swimming!' It didn't matter. He would have gone to the opening of a bottle of aspirin. And it made me think—little things, little moments. Go for them."

In 1991 cancer hit even closer to home when she contracted breast cancer and underwent a mastectomy of her left breast. When she finally got up the courage to show her husband, Bill, the incision, she expected him to be repulsed. "I searched his face carefully for his reaction," she wrote later. "There was nothing there but love."

One year later, in July of 1993, both kidneys shut down, so she started four-times-a-day peritoneal dialysis and, refusing preferential treatment, went on a list for a kidney transplant.

In one column she told of a recurring dream.

She was standing before God and He said to her, "So empty your pockets. What have you got left of your life? Any dreams that were unfulfilled? Any unused talent that I gave you when you were born that you still have left? Any unsaid compliments or bits of love that you haven't spread around?" And she answered, "I've nothing to return. I spent everything You gave me. I'm as naked as the day I was born."

On April 3, 1996, she was rushed to San Francisco's University of California Medical Center for a kidney transplant. At first it was declared a success. But then complications set in. On the morning of April 22, Erma Bombeck died of heart failure. She was 69.

Every time I walk by my friend's fridge, I am reminded of Erma's gentle spunk and wit. And I am reminded that those who turn their back on self-pity and choose joy enrich not only their own life. They enrich the world.

"Lord," I pray, "if I can't be wealthy, make me rich in laughter and friends. If I can't be healthy, give me strength for today. If You won't take my troubles away, at least give me joy to face them.

"Until the day I stand before You. Having spent everything You gave me. With nothing left but a smile."

CHAPTER EIGHT

I Beg Your Pardon

"Circumstances and situations do color life, but you have been given the mind to choose what the color shall be."

—JOHN HOMER MILLER (1722–1791)

THIS PAST WINTER, THANKS TO A MISCHIEVOUS weatherman and an unending snowfall, we did something a little unusual at our house. After two weeks of brutally cold temperatures and the diagnosis of more to come, we decided to brighten the winter blues with a trip to our town's indoor swimming pool. After pumping ourselves up with excitement, however, we were a little deflated to discover that the car wouldn't start. My eldest son was so mad he wanted to set it on fire (something which would have given us all a degree of satisfaction).

Instead I herded the troops back inside and told them I had something else in mind. Something special. "You sit here and listen," I said. "And see if you can guess what it is." Grabbing a shovel, I propped a ladder against the house and climbed onto our gently sloping roof. The kids watched in awe as the heaviest snowfall in history fell past our kitchen window.

Soon, I'd shoveled a six-foot pile of snow into the backyard. Before long, we were having the time of our lives jumping off the roof into what looked like a giant homemade marshmallow. We hollered. We shouted. We threw snowballs. We pretended we were sky divers and stuntmen. We even pretended we were warm.

And afterward, sitting around a heat vent and drinking hot chocolate thick with marshmallows, we all agreed: Plan B was better than Plan A. "I like winter best of all," said Rachael. "We never drink hot chocolate in the summer."

Of course, not everyone feels this way about the cold. The following diary entries tell the story of a Southerner who moves north to sample the marvels of a white Christmas and ends up getting a little more than he bargained for.

A SOUTHERNER MOVES NORTH

Dear Diary:

December 8 It's starting to snow. The first of the season and the first we've seen in years. The wife and I took our hot chocolate and sat by the picture window watching the snowflakes drift down, cling to the trees, then cover the ground. Ah, it was beautiful!

December 9 Awoke to a lovely blanket of crystal white snow covering the landscape. What a fantastic sight! Every tree and shrub covered with a beautiful white mantle. I shoveled snow for the first time in years and loved every minute of it! I did both our driveway and our sidewalk. Later, a city snowplow came along and accidentally covered up our drive-way with compacted snow. The driver smiled and waved. I waved back and shoveled again.

December 10 It snowed an additional five inches last night and the temperature dropped to around 11 degrees. Several limbs on the trees and shrubs snapped due to the weight of the snow. I shoveled our driveway again. Shortly afterward, the snowplow driver came by and did his trick again.

December 11 Warmed up enough today to create some slush, which soon became ice when the temperature dropped again. Bought snow tires for both cars—almost 800 dollars. Fell on my rear in the driveway—145 dollars for chiropractor. Thankfully nothing was broken. More snow and ice expected.

December 12 Still cold. Sold the wife's car and bought a 4 × 4 to get her to work. Slid into a guardrail and did considerable damage to the right rear panel. Had another eight inches of the white crud last night. Both vehicles covered in salt and sludge. More shoveling in store. That idiot snowplow came by twice today!

December 13 Two degrees outside. More stupid snow. Not a tree or shrub on our property that hasn't been damaged. Power off most of the night. Tried to keep from freezing to death with candles and a kerosene heater, which tipped over and nearly burned the house down. I managed to put the flames out, but suffered second-degree burns on my hands and lost all my eyebrows and eyelashes. Car slid on the ice on the way to the emergency room and did more damage.

December 14 Stupid white junk keeps coming down! Have to put on all the clothes we own just to go to the stupid mailbox! If I ever catch the son-of-a-gun who drives the snowplow, I'll chew open his chest and rip out his heart! I think he hides around the corner and waits till I finish shoveling and then comes down the street at 100 M.P.H. Power still off. Toilet frozen. Part of the roof has started to cave in.

December 15 Six more stupid inches of stupid snow and stupid sleet and stupid ice and who knows what other kind of white crud fell last night! I wounded the snowplow idiot with an ice ax, but he got away. Wife left me. Car won't start. I think I'm going snow-blind. Can't move my toes. Haven't seen the sun in weeks. More snow predicted. Forget this! I'm moving back to Mississippi.

———

I love that story because, to one degree or another, we've all been there, haven't we?

I once read of a missionary mother with a mentally handicapped child whom she handled with grace and patience. Every time this little guy ate, he got more food where he wasn't supposed to than where he was. And every time he finished eating, his mother cleaned up the mess without complaining. It was a little like a reenactment of the feeding of the 5000. Each day she gave him a small helping, and when he was finished she cleaned up 12 baskets full of remnants! But during breakfast one hot summer day, things were worse than usual. When she had to duck to avoid getting hit by a syrupy pancake, the usually patient mother came unglued.

After she stopped yelling, her little boy slowly lifted his head, looked at her with big blue eyes, and sang a song he'd heard on the radio: "I beg your pardon, I never promised you a rose garden."[6]

Her anger vanished, and before long the two of them were laughing.

What that precious little guy was telling his mom was one of the most profound things either of them would ever learn: "Hey, Ma, life is gonna throw some wild things your way. But keep your head up. It can make all the difference."

So it is with us. In the dead of winter . . . on a hot summer day . . . rich people choose well their attitude. You see, the richest people I know don't always understand what is going on. They don't always like what they see. But they have a quiet confidence that God will put all things together for their good.

When I think of rich people, I think of the apostle Paul. In the midst of pressures, disappointments, and prison life, he challenged us to:

> Rejoice in the Lord always. I will say it again: Rejoice! Let your gentleness be evident to all. The Lord is near. Do not be anxious about anything, but in everything, by prayer and petition, with thanksgiving, present your requests to God. And the peace of God, which transcends all understanding, will guard your hearts and your minds in Christ Jesus (Philippians 4:4-7).

Paul knew that things were bad all over. He knew that life wasn't fair. He also knew that while he couldn't control his circumstances, the one thing he could control was his attitude—he could pray and choose an attitude of joy.

When a simple phone call changed my life one April morning, I began to learn this lesson the hard way.

CHAPTER NINE

Daddy, Is Momma Gonna Die?

"With profound potential for good, suffering can also be a destroyer. Suffering can pull families together, uniting them through hardship, or it can rip them apart in selfishness and bitterness. . . . It all depends. On us. On how we respond."

—Joni Eareckson Tada

I WAS WRITING A HUMOR COLUMN ON MONEY and marriage when the phone rang. Letting it ring, I finished the sentence. "Someone stole my VISA card, but I haven't reported it yet. You see, the thief is spending less than my wife."

Then I picked up the receiver: "Hello."

There was silence at first, then the words I've never forgotten. Words that made my stomach tighten and my heart pound. "H-h-help me, please help me, I don't know what's happening—"

Normally it's a five-minute jog from my office to our house, but I'm sure I was there in two. Bursting through the front door, I found the kids on the kitchen floor pouring oatmeal into a stainless steel bowl. "Daddy, is Momma gonna die?" asked the eldest, five-year-old Stephen.

On the living-room couch lay Ramona, my wife of nine years. An ugly gash ran up her left leg and blood had stained the carpet. Staring up at me with vacant eyes, she asked, "What day is it? It's Monday, isn't it?"

It was Friday, to be precise. April 10, 1992. The first day of a journey down a road we would not have chosen.

———

Until that day, life had been a bowl of cherries with few pits. Although we'd had three kids in three years, we couldn't have been happier. I often joked with Ramona: "Sure we have three small kids, but we're far more satisfied than the guy who has three million dollars." "How so?" she asked. "Well, the guy with three million wants more!"

The truth is, we were very satisfied. We had everything we'd ever dreamed of. A close family. An improving marriage. And to make matters better, my first book had just been accepted by a major publisher.

Early in January of 1992, however, things began to change. Waking up in the middle of the night, I would find Ramona pacing the floor. "What's wrong?" I'd ask. "I'm fine," she'd reply. "I just can't sleep."

Finally one night she broke down and told me the reason: "I'm hardly sleeping. I'm thinking about this disease that's in my family."

The disease was Huntington's, a rare neurological disorder that had haunted her since she learned about it in her early teens. On the scale of human misery, the disease ranks high, bringing mental and physical deterioration, then nursing homes and life-support systems. "My dad had it before he drowned, and I have a 50/50 chance of getting it," she told me when we were dating. "I thought you should know, before we get . . . any further along." My response was the last thing she expected: "I'd like to marry you someday, Ramona. I love you." After that I never gave the disease much thought. *We're young,* I convinced myself. *We're invincible.*

But by the time our kids were born, three of Ramona's six siblings had been diagnosed with Huntington's and she thought she was next. The symptoms were there: lack of sleep, irritability, occasional clumsiness, even a craving for sweets.

On the day of the phone call, she awoke at eight o'clock feeling rather dizzy. The last thing she remembers is standing up to pull on her housecoat. And as she fell, her leg struck the corner of our wooden bed frame.

———

Quickly I wrapped Ramona's wound and headed for the kitchen. "What happened to Mommy?" I asked Stephen, who was stirring oatmeal while his two-year-old brother added a generous handful of salt.

"I don't know," he answered. "She was making funny noises and she didn't talk right. She thinks I'm her dad."

Gathering the three of them into my arms, I held them tightly. "Maybe we should tell Jesus," said Rachael, who was three. "Maybe He can do something." Holding them close, I prayed out loud: "Dear God, help Mommy to be okay. And thank You that You're right here with us all the time."

"Daddy," said Rachael, pulling on my ear, "can we have *bweakfast* now?"

As the children munched cold cereal, I called my parents who lived nearby. "Mom," I said, "I'm not sure what's wrong with Ramona. She's not doing too great. Can you take the kids for a while? And . . . can you pray?" Then I phoned Ramona's mother. Half an hour later she arrived with a warm hug and an optimistic smile. But the smile soon faded. "You sure it's Friday?" Ramona kept asking her. "It can't be."

I was standing in the living room flipping through a phone book for the number of our doctor. Suddenly Ramona's back arched. Her head snapped back. And an agonizing moan escaped her lips. Her face—an ashen gray—tightened, and her body slumped to the floor. Quickly I rolled her over to keep her from choking. "Dial 9-1-1!" I yelled. On the floor, Ramona thrashed her arms and legs, but no breath would come. Grabbing her arms to keep her from hurting herself, I prayed, "Oh God, please, please—"

It was the first seizure I'd ever witnessed. It would be the first of hundreds.

The cost of the 90-minute ambulance ride to a nearby city was the least of my worries as we weaved in and out of busy traffic. My high-school sweetheart lay before me, unconscious. Was this the beginning of Huntington's? Or the end of everything? I clutched her hand tightly. Beside me sat a Christian nurse, a childhood friend. "I remember reading an interview with Linda Ronstadt once," I told her. "She said, 'I'll never get married, there's too much potential for pain.' I . . . I guess I finally understand what she meant."

My friend put her hand on mine. "Ah yes," she replied, "but you would never have known such joy either." Tears slid down my cheeks and I didn't bother wiping them away.

———

In the hospital, the endless battery of tests began. CTs. EEGs. You name it, they scanned it. "They scanned my brain and found nothing?" joked Ramona on the morning of the fourth day. I laughed, bent over, and kissed her face. But the outlook wasn't so funny. Doctors, psychologists, and neurologists each had a different opinion. "This has nothing to do with Huntington's," said one. "I believe she's having pseudoseizures. She'll get over it." A veteran psychologist told us that because Ramona had watched her father drown when she was eight, she was probably reliving the trauma. "It's called Post Traumatic Stress Disorder," he told me. "Counseling is the answer."

Back home, our doctor diagnosed her with severe depression and recommended an antidepressant. When I went to pick up the pills, the pharmacist took me aside. "Phil," he said, holding up the pill bottle, "these things were part of the reason my first marriage ended. My wife became a different person when she started taking them. All I can say is, don't let it happen to you. I thought divorce would cure my problems. I was wrong."

During the next few weeks Ramona seemed to improve. My boss graciously allowed me to carry on my editorial duties at home, and at night after everyone was asleep I put the finishing touches on my book *Honey, I Dunked the Kids.* In a chapter called "Surprise, Surprise," I told the story of our youngest son, Jeffrey, born a mere 51 weeks after his sister. "God's grace always accompanies life's surprises," I wrote.

I had no idea how tightly I would clutch those words in the days that lay ahead.

CHAPTER TEN

Surprise Endings

*"I know God will not give me anything I can't handle.
I just wish He wouldn't trust me so much."*

—MOTHER TERESA (1910–1997)

IN MARCH OF 1993, THE GENE THAT CAUSES Huntington's was discovered at last. And so, one year after the seizures began, we drove to a nearby city for a simple blood test. "We'll be in touch," the nurse told us. But weeks of waiting turned to months. Finally I called the Huntington's clinic. "Why so long?" I asked. "This is a little-known disease," came the response. "Public interest is minimal and there isn't much government funding. We have only a few people working on it and we've got a tremendous backlog. We're sorry."

In July, my book came out and was an overnight success. Work began on a sequel: *Daddy, I Blew Up the Shed.* I remember sitting in my study doing radio interviews, trying to cheer people up. "How can you laugh when life ain't so funny?" one talk-show host asked me. I talked about our present situation. How our lives could not be described as happy ones, but strangely there were moments that were jam-packed with joy. "Joy," I said, "does not depend on sunny circumstances, on good news or happy endings. It comes from knowing that whatever happens, God loves me; that whatever happens, He is preparing a better place for those who love Him."

When we paused for commercials I would put down the phone and run to the next room to check on my wife.

In January of 1994, the test results were finally in. We could come hear about them on February 14. *Come on,* I thought, *that's a day for parties, not final verdicts.* Then I realized how fitting it was. You see, on our wedding day, I stood before 300 witnesses and God Himself, promising to be her sweetheart no matter what came our way. On each Valentine's Day since I had renewed that vow. "Besides," I told Ramona one day, "we have to stay together. I've put on so much weight since we were married that I can't get my wedding ring off."

The night before Valentine's Day, a group of friends held a party for us. We prayed together, laughed together, and cried together. These were the ones who had been there during those ten months. They didn't have all the answers. They simply had a little time. Time to listen to music. Time to talk. Time to play Scrabble.

On February 14, 1994, two doctors held the test results in a small envelope. At last one tore it open and looked over her glasses at us: "Ramona, you have the normal gene." At first I didn't know what she meant. The normal gene. The normal Huntington's gene. Soon my wife would be an invalid. Then the doctor said, "Which means you don't have Huntington's." We stood together in disbelief.

"We don't have it?"

"You don't have it."

Hugging two doctors, we thanked them profusely. Ramona was clear. The disease could not be passed on to our children. That night we celebrated the happiest day of our lives with dinner at a seafood restaurant and a movie with friends. We had finally broken through a long, dark tunnel. Surely now the seizures would end.

As the months dragged by, however, the seizures worsened. "Things will get better," our doctor kept telling us. "It just takes time." But by 1996, time seemed to be running out.

A mere 90 pounds now, Ramona had no appetite and rarely left the house. When she did, people in our small town barely recognized her. One day as we drove to visit her sister, a seizure laid her flat out in the front seat beside me. Terrified, the children cowered in the backseat, crying. I comforted them as best I could, and after our arrival, took them to a nearby McDonald's. "How do you guys feel?" I asked. "Scared," came the reply. "Is Mommy gonna die?"

"I don't know, kids," I said. "Sometimes I'm scared too. But you know what? God said He'll always be with us. And He's never broken a promise. You can tell Him when you're scared. And you can tell me too, okay?" I didn't know if I'd said the right thing, but soon the kids were laughing and enjoying their cheeseburgers.

By this time we had seen 21 specialists, scoured libraries for literature, and tried to diagnose the problem ourselves. Well-meaning friends suggested that demonic activity was involved, so we sought godly counsel. Our pastors prayed over Ramona, anointing her with oil. For months she met twice a week with a female counselor, but still the seizures continued.

Every night we lay awake in the darkness, unable to sleep. And sometimes panic overtook me. "What do I do now, Lord? Where do we go from here?" There was only silence. The windows of heaven were shut, it seemed. The shutters drawn tight.

Then verses my mother had drummed into me when I was a child came back to comfort us. "God is my refuge and strength, an ever present help in trouble, therefore we will not fear though the earth give way and the mountains fall into the heart of the sea . . ." "'I know the plans I have for you,' declares the Lord, 'plans to give you a hope and a future.'"

But by the fall of 1996, even hope was slipping from my grasp. The seizures were occurring every day and sometimes every half hour. I rarely left Ramona's side now, and late one night, after she was finally asleep, I paced our darkened backyard and fell to my knees pounding the ground. "God," I cried, "I can't take it anymore. Please do something."

I would love to tell you that I saw handwriting in the sky or heard an audible voice. But instead, as I stood to my feet, a doctor's name came to mind. We attended the same church, but I'd never thought to ask Dan his opinion. A few minutes later I had him on the phone. After listening to my description, he said simply, "I've seen this once before. It sounds like she has a chemical deficiency. Bring her to me first thing in the morning. There's a new drug to treat it."

I don't know if I really believed in miracles before that point in my life. But within a week, Ramona was a different person. Her eyes lit up with the sparkle that first attracted me to her. The seizures ended. God had given me my wife back.

Of course, we're not home yet. There are more tests ahead. But every day my wife wakes up beside the most thankful guy in the world. I'm thankful that God's grace *does* accompany life's surprises. That in the toughest of times His grace can help us choose joy over bitterness, and help us stay together when our whole world is falling apart.

Oh yes, you may be wondering about the VISA card joke I was writing out the day a phone call changed my life. The truth is, it's a lie. I am far richer because I met this girl. In fact, the only thing she's stolen is my heart.

CHAPTER ELEVEN

The Angel Jeffrey

"A world without children is a world without newness, regeneration, color, and vigor."

—JAMES C. DOBSON

IN NOVEMBER OF 1997 MY PHONE BEGAN RINGING off the hook. "I guess you're famous," said one member of the media. "I am?" I replied. "Not you," he laughed, "your town. It's the birthplace of Bobbi McCaughey, the most famous mother in the world. You know, the mother of the septuplets."

By noon that day, three television crews had arrived. For some reason the town office had put them in touch with me, and before long I was fielding questions in the glare of the bright lights. "Do you remember Bobbi very well?" one reporter asked. "As a matter of fact," I told him, "we dated for four years." His eyes lit up. "But we broke up. She wanted too many kids." His eyes were wider than ever, so I informed him that it was a joke, or it might have made the evening news.

The lights dimmed, but the questions persisted. National newspapers and magazines wanted to know if our small town would be naming a street after Bobbi. "Yes," I said, "it's called Seventh Street." Were the births a miracle? How could I respond otherwise? After all, I watched our three come into the world one at a time, and it's a wonder their mother lived. If I had to go through this process, I would require so much medication that I wouldn't wake up until the kids were in grade four.

That night when we turned on the evening news, there I was. "We had three kids in three years and I thought we had it tough," I said. "Bobbi had seven in six minutes. She could use a little help and a lot of prayer."

Whether you had your children one at a time or not, I'm sure you would agree with me that an attitude of thankfulness and a good sense of humor are keys to keeping your sanity.

If you listen to your children long enough, you'll find plenty to laugh about. One day I overheard one child explaining to another, "My mom can't have any more kids because her tubes are tired."

When Jeffrey (our youngest) was only four, I endeavored to remove him single-handedly from a Sunday-morning worship service. He was creating quite a stir, judging from the way everyone in the church building was looking at me, so I picked him up and whisked him swiftly toward the back doors of the church. As I did, Jeffrey hollered: "Pray for me!"

That same year, we invited a prestigious Bible scholar over for supper. Jeffrey seemed to enjoy his company and when the man asked, "What would you like to be when you grow up?" Jeffrey put down his fork. "A baseball player, a hockey player, and a football player," he replied. "What would you like to be when you grow up?"

The scholar smiled. "A teacher," he said. Jeffrey sized him up and said, "But you don't know anything." Thankfully our friend thought this was the funniest thing he'd heard in a long time.

Jeffrey is eight now, but still he loves to tell it the way it is. Why shouldn't he? His older brother, Stephen, has pointed the way. A few months ago in Sunday school his teacher was talking about Solomon. About his great gift of wisdom. And his great list of wives. Stephen thought for a minute, raised his hand, and said: "Wow! He must have had one BIG bed!"

I love the honesty of children. And sometimes, though I hate to admit it, they're far more perceptive than adults.

The other night we boys were sitting together on our small couch watching the playoffs. Now that Jeffrey's of age, I occasionally let him control the remote. Three or four seconds into an advertisement he decides if it should go on or "be zapped." Five seconds after he zaps it, he reconsiders. "Dad," said Jeffrey, squeezing the power button, "I know why they call 'em ads. Because they keep adding stuff on that isn't true." I'd never heard a better definition.

About then the phone rang. "Hello?"

"Yes . . . Phil, it's Alexia. We're putting together the Mother's Day service on Sunday . . . and we were wondering if you could get Jeffrey to say a few words about his mom."

"Uh, you're kidding, aren't you? Why don't we just send in the clowns?"

Alexia was serious. "Come on, Phil. He'll do just fine."

"Well . . . sure . . . why not?" I agreed, then hung up and thought of several reasons.

On Sunday, I sat beside Jeffrey, wondering if we should have put a little more thought into his speech. After all, the rest of the children were older and gave carefully rehearsed eulogies: "My mom is Ruth Graham, Susanna Wesley, Mother Teresa, and Cindy Crawford all rolled into a trim 110 pounds. She can outcook, outclean, outshop, outwash just about anything on two legs. And I would just like to say that without her, I wouldn't be here to give this speech which my father prepared so carefully late last night."

When Jeffrey's turn arrived, I realized we hadn't written anything, so I went along to lend some support. Picking up the microphone, I said, "Well, that Mrs. Leo is something, isn't she, Jeffrey? How about your mom?"

For the first time in eight years, he was speechless.

"What do you like about Mom?" I asked.

"Um . . . she cooks food for us," said Jeffrey. "Sometimes."

This brought no small degree of pleasure to the audience.

"So is she the best mom you've ever had?"

"Yep."

"Do you have anything else to say about Mommy?"

"Nope."

I was really hoping for more than this. Something like, "Mom, you're the best invention since rollerblades. When I needed a shoulder, a hug, or a diaper, you had one. When Dad was sleeping, you were awake. You carried me for nine months, and you haven't let me down since. I love you, Mom."

Instead he said, "Nope." And we sat down.

Forgive me, Pastor John, but I can't remember the message. I was too busy squeezing my wife's hand and thanking God that though her kids haven't yet risen publicly to bless her, they often do so in private.

I thought back to the cold January morning when this same little boy was only four. Each morning in those days he awoke and made a beeline for the dress-up box at the end of the hall. After pulling on a Superman cape, a hat, and a belt, he would get down on all fours and chase his brother and sister throughout the house. "I'm a kissing bull," he told them. They loved every terrifying minute of it.

On this particular morning, Jeffrey charged into our bedroom and gave his mom a hug. Looking up, he noticed tears streaming down her face. He couldn't have known that she had just received a shattering phone call, and that she faced an uncertain future. He couldn't know that she'd already spent nine months waiting to hear the results of the blood test for Huntington's disease. But he knew enough to pass on the best news he'd ever heard. And so, as only a four-year-old can, he sang:

I will not be afraid for God is with me.

This he sang three times.

An angel dressed up like a kissing bull.

Sometimes wacky. Sometimes wonderful. These are the gifts God gives. Our tubes may be tired, but we couldn't be more thankful.

Part III

RICH PEOPLE ARE PEOPLE PEOPLE

When asked what has made life rich, more than 90 percent of the respondents to my survey used one word: relationships. Relationships with friends and spouses, children and grandchildren.

"Friendship is the greatest of worldly goods," believed C. S. Lewis. "If I had to give a piece of advice to a young man about a place to live, I think I should say, 'sacrifice almost everything to live where you can be near your friends.'"

At its best, companionship deepens our joy, lightens our load, and brightens our path. But, let's face it, friendships end. Marriages dissolve. People disappoint. Movie star Judy Garland once told a reporter, "If I'm such a legend, then why am I so lonely? Let me tell you, legends are all very well if you've got somebody around who loves you."

Perhaps you feel like Judy. You've carried the burden of failure. You've felt the brush of disappointment. Or perhaps you just long to make a good thing better. Either way, these stories are for you. May they help us realize that the best things in life may be closer than we think.

CHAPTER TWELVE

Life, Love, and Hot Dogs

"A man travels the world over in search of what he needs and returns home to find it."

—GEORGE MOORE (1852–1933)

ON MONDAY MORNING MY WIFE LEFT ME. PACKED up some earthly belongings, our only daughter, and a VISA card (this time I'm telling the truth), then headed west for a week, leaving Jeffrey (8), Stephen (11), and me (a little older) to fend for ourselves. For her this was good. She deserved a break. She deserved to surround herself with mountains and siblings and hot springs. But for me? Well . . . let me say that during the last few days I have developed a new theory. If you're a theologian you may disagree with me, but here goes:

I think God invented Eve mainly to help Adam find things.

Adam would be walking around saying, "Let me see . . . where did I put those figs?" and none of the animals would tell him. So, after God stopped laughing, He thought, *This guy can do without a rib, but not without a wife.* Ever since, men have been pursuing women, largely because they need help finding things: "Honey, do you remember where we parked the silver Winnebago?"

In the last week I have visited the fridge roughly 450 times and found nothing there. Oh sure, there's milk. There's Parmesan cheese. There's olive oil. But where are the sandwiches? Where's the lasagna? These are the things meals are made of.

My son Stephen ran out of socks on Tuesday, and we're not sure where fresh ones come from. I can't find my wife's list of meal suggestions. Jeffrey can't find any more shirts, so he wears the same one 24 hours a day. It has a very interesting design. This shirt can tell you what we've eaten for the last five days. Mostly we've eaten pizza. Sometimes we order it in. If we're really hungry we go get it. For breakfast we eat Fruit Hoops, which have all the nutritional value of steel-belted radials. For lunch, I phone friends and tell them my wife is gone, then weep openly. So far no one seems to care. The girls will come home and find us flat out on the carpet: pale, emaciated, gasping. "We couldn't find the Rolaids," are the last words we'll utter.

On Thursday we went to a baseball game and consumed our weight in hot dogs. The box told us they contained "actual meat products," which was certainly a comfort. After the final out Jeffrey rubbed his tummy and asked, "When's Mom coming home?"

"In six more meals," I told him. He rolled his eyes and let out the cutest little burp.

What I didn't tell him is that, although she promised to return Sunday, she is the mother of three young children and has a husband who can't find anything, so we may not see her until Jeffrey's high-school graduation. I also did not tell him that even as we speak she's probably sitting in the hot springs swapping childbirth stories with her sisters and saying, "They thought I was coming home Sunday. Can you imagine? Just how insane do they think I am?" And then the mountains would echo with crazed laughter.

———

On Friday I went to a convenience store to pick up the necessities of life: some pop, some chips, a Rocky video. Standing in line, I felt a tap on the shoulder. It was a classmate from high school. We exchanged handshakes. "How's it going?" he asked. "Oh, man," I said, laughing, "my wife's gone for a week, so I'm here to pick up some health food. Life's been a little wild lately."

He looked down and kicked at a floor tile.

"How about you?" I asked.

"Well, not so good. My wife's . . . well . . . she's been gone on a more permanent basis. She left a year ago, you know . . ." His voice trailed away as a little girl peeked out from behind him.

"I'm sorry," I said, embarrassed. "I didn't mean to . . . I'm sorry."

———

As I write these words, I'm sitting alone at a computer, thinking about life. About love. About grace.

You see, Friday night after I got home from the convenience store, I searched through the freezer looking for ice cream. I found some. And to my surprise I found a whole lot more. Lasagna. Homemade buns. All-beef hot dogs. My wife had put them there for us. I hadn't found the note she left.

I guess that's life.

Sometimes the best things we'll ever have were there all along.

CHAPTER THIRTEEN

---◉---

Your Own Backyard

"I'd rather laugh in a tent than cry in a palace."

—BILL JENSEN

MANY YEARS AGO, AMID THE SEARING HEAT OF an African summer, a farmer stopped plowing his field and stood wiping his brow, squinting at the horizon. In the distance, a small band of adventurers—much like the one he had seen a few minutes ago—was heading for the mountains.

If only I could join them, he thought.

Since the discovery of diamonds, thousands of people were dropping everything to join the search for the valuable stones. But not the farmer. There was work to be done. Fields to be tilled. Livestock to be fed. Yet the promise of great wealth kept him awake at night and turned his menial tasks to drudgery. One day when a complete stranger offered to buy his farm, the farmer agreed with a handshake.

At last he was free. Free to pursue his dream.

The search was long and painful. Trekking mile after weary mile across deserts and plains, through jungles and mountain passes, the farmer searched for the elusive diamonds. But none could be found. The weeks turned to months, and the months to years. Finally, penniless, sick, and utterly depressed, he took his own life by throwing himself into a raging river.

Back home, the man who had purchased the farm carefully tilled the land. One day as he was planting a crop, he came across a strange-looking stone. Carrying it to the farmhouse, he placed it on the mantel.

That very night, a friend noticed the unusual stone over the fireplace and picked it up, turning it over and over in his hands. Then, with wide eyes, he turned to the new owner of the farm and said, "Do you know what you have here? This has to be one of the largest diamonds ever found."

Further investigation proved him right. And before long it was discovered that the entire farm was literally covered with similar magnificent stones. The farm sold by the first farmer turned out to be one of the richest, most productive diamond mines in the world.[7]

The times haven't changed much, have they? Just like the man who was so quick to sell the farm, too few of us take the time to investigate and polish what we already have. In our disappointment with the way things are, in our quest to get ahead, we fail to recognize the wealth in our own backyard. And we end up walking over untold riches every day.

Recently I met Andrew. A successful insurance and investment consultant, he spent the last 20 years of his life "searching for diamonds." Eighteen months ago, he made his way back home. But by then, his house was empty. His wife of 23 years had taken their teenage son and daughter and moved 1000 miles away, leaving Andrew with a sprawling ranch, two speedboats, and an antique car collection. "I have absolutely everything," he told me. "It's all paid for. But I've never been so empty. I didn't know what I had, until it was gone."

Six months ago, suicidal and desperate, Andrew fell to his knees and prayed, asking Jesus Christ to change him. To forgive him of the past and help him face the future. "This may sound crazy," he told me, "but since that day I have experienced more peace than I did during all those years of success. In many ways, my life is the most chaotic it has ever been, but every morning I take my worries and concerns to the living room and I spend an hour on my knees trying to leave them with God. Sometimes I find myself picking them up again during the day, but I'm learning to trust Him to take care of my family just like He's taking care of me."

Today Andrew is doing all he can to reconcile with his wife and children, but he knows the road ahead is steep. "I thought I was giving them everything they needed," he says. "I guess what they really needed was me."

When I told Andrew about the book I was writing, he said, "Tell people about the riches of relationships. I was so busy building an empire I forgot to build a home. I was so busy working on multimillion-dollar deals that I hardly had time to buy my friends a cup of coffee. I would trade all this stuff in a heartbeat for one good friendship."

I wish I could turn the clock back for Andrew. And sometimes I'd like to turn it back for myself. But like Andrew, I'm learning that it is relationships, not ranches, that make men rich. I'm learning that we make a living by what we get. We make a life by what we give.

"But, Phil," you may be saying, "you don't know my family. You don't know my friends. Hey, these people aren't just diamonds in the rough. They're big chunks of coal."

You may be right, but before you decide, let me tell you about two friends of mine. Two friends I had filed neatly into the coal category. Until some unique circumstances changed things for good.

CHAPTER FOURTEEN

A Tale of Two Friends

"Life is to be fortified by many friendships. To love and to be loved is the greatest happiness of existence."
—SYDNEY SMITH (1771–1845)

KEVIN BIRCH AND I GREW UP TOGETHER IN THE same little town. But we seldom bumped into each other outside the hockey rink. And believe me, when we met there, sparks sometimes flew.

In high school, I took up refereeing. Still don't know why. Perhaps I wanted to learn a few lessons about the depravity of man. One night, while refereeing a game, I watched Kevin (who was not a dentist) attempt to remove the teeth of a fellow sportsman. After stopping the play, I informed him of his crime, and invited him to spend two minutes in the penalty box thinking of mending his ways.

Skating toward the penalty box, Kevin let me know that I had serious problems with my eyesight, that my nose was crooked, and that there were some pretty bad people on my family tree. In other words, the air matched his uniform: a deep blue. While reporting the penalty to the timekeeper, I thought of making Kevin sit a while longer, perhaps four to six years, but instead I grinned at him. "So you didn't like my call, huh?" He shook his head, then surprised me. "Callaway," he said, "I'm sorry. I need to talk to you. I'll wait for you after the game."

I had heard this from other players. I had heard this from parents. But following the game, Kevin approached me with good intentions. "It's been quite a week," he said, apologizing again. "Do you have a few minutes to talk?" Over a tall glass of Coke in a nearby restaurant, he told me of his struggle with friends, with substance abuse, and with God. I don't know if I said much that night that was helpful. All I did was listen. When Kevin informed me that he was finished with his faith in God, I said, "Well, if you ever need a religious fanatic to talk to, you know where to find me." We laughed together. And during the next few years, he often took me up on my offer.

Sometimes, late at night, the phone would ring and Kevin would be desperate. "I need you to pray for me. Things aren't going so well." And while he listened at the other end of the line, I would pray.

Fifteen years have passed and I've watched him come back to God. I've also watched him become one of my best friends on the face of the earth. He's a farmer by trade, and when he's out steering a tractor, you'll probably find him praying with his eyes open. "I pray for you," he tells me, "when I remember to. I'm not the best at remembering, but I try."

Sometimes when I travel, I ask Kevin to come along. Sitting on a plane bound for Toronto recently, he finally got up enough nerve to ask me a question he'd been pondering for years: "How did your nose get so crooked?"

"When I was in ninth grade I weighed less than 100 pounds," I told him. "So I started lifting weights. One day I was bench-pressing 40 pounds and my arms gave way. Guess where the barbells landed?"

Kevin laughed until I thought he would need the oxygen mask.

The very next day while sightseeing at the CN Tower, the world's largest freestanding structure, Kevin turned to say something to me and walked nose-first into a huge sliding-glass door. He hit it so hard he knocked it off its hinges. We spent the afternoon in a nearby hospital where I watched a doctor push, pull, and prod that nose until he was satisfied it wasn't broken. "If it wasn't broken before," Kevin said on our way out, "it is now."

By the time we headed for home, his nose was twice the size of normal. Black shadows had formed around his eyes. He looked like a raccoon who had taken up boxing. "I feel your pain," I told him. "Good friends do that." We talked about our friendship then, and of the time we met outside the penalty box.

"I wonder where I'd be if you'd thrown me out of the game that night," Kevin said, looking out the window at the setting sun.

I'm not sure where I would be either.

You see, after we got home, a doctor informed Kevin that his nose was broken for sure. In fact, if you saw us standing together, you'd swear we had the same plastic surgeon.

Every time Kevin looks in the mirror now, he has a small reminder of me. And every time he hesitates before opening a glass door, he smiles and says a prayer for his friend with the crooked nose.

CHAPTER FIFTEEN

Two Men and a Lawnmower

"Every man should keep a fair-sized cemetery in which to bury the faults of his friends."

—HENRY WARD BEECHER (1813–1887)

IF FIRST IMPRESSIONS ARE EVERYTHING, THEN we were both in trouble. My new neighbor, Vance, had just flung a sarcastic remark in my direction and I'd returned it with equal skill. If we had been playing tennis, it would have made for an interesting match, but as it was there was no love lost here. Believe me, neither of us would have wagered that one day we would become life-long friends.

Our friendship began with the death of my electric lawnmower. After burying it in a yard sale, I began looking around for a new one. Sure enough, one Saturday while gazing through Vance's fence, I noticed to my delight that he had a blue gas-powered lawnmower that worked. To my surprise, he agreed to lend it. And that's where our friendship started.

And almost ended. Looking back now, I'm amazed that he stuck with me.

Especially after what happened the second time I borrowed it.

Vance was gone that sunny Saturday, so, climbing the fence, I pushed the lawnmower back to my yard, and began trimming the grass.

For some reason I was in a hurry that day, so when I came to a large stump which protruded two inches from the ground, I thought I would conserve time by going over it rather than around it. This was a gas-powered lawnmower, I reasoned. It would clear The Stump without a problem. I was wrong. BAAAMM! The mower stopped dead, never to start again. The starting mechanism would not even move.

My father always taught me what to do in such a situation. "Son, when you borrow something," he said, "always return it." So I carefully pushed the lawnmower into the exact spot from which it was taken. Then I left on a five-day business trip.

Upon my return, Vance was waiting. In fact, as I pulled into the driveway he was standing nearby, a rather serious expression etched on his face.

"Hi, Vance!" I said, warmly.

"Come with me," he said, without any warmth at all. Obediently I followed him to the backyard and straight over to The Stump. Surrounding it was a "Police Line Do Not Cross" yellow ribbon. And on the ground in white paint: the outline of a lawnmower.

"We have a suspect," said Vance, smiling at last.

Then he took me to the garden, where—I kid you not—handlebars protruded from a fresh mound of earth. Taped to a large gray brick were these words:

Here lies Mr. Mower
1982–1992
A life so quickly taken
By a hand so quick to take
He will never mow
What life had
In the grass ahead of him.

It's not hard to understand why we're the best of friends today. You see, if I need some advice, a good laugh, or someone to listen, I call Vance. For one thing, Vance knows how to practice the fine art of forgiveness. He also knows what every good friend knows: If you expect perfection from people, your whole life will be a series of disappointments, grumblings, and complaints. But if you lower your expectations a little and accept people as the imperfect creatures that we all are, you just may find yourself a lifelong friend.

Our story doesn't end there. You see, after the death of his blue lawnmower, Vance's wife went down to a hardware store and entered a drawing for a nice new red one. And—you guessed it—she won.

Today, all because of me, they have a shiny red lawnmower in their backyard.

I haven't tried borrowing it yet.

But I do keep reminding Vance just how lucky he is to have me for a friend.

CHAPTER SIXTEEN

Seven Secrets to Great Friendships

"I am wealthy in my friends."
—WILLIAM SHAKESPEARE (1564–1616)

HAVE YOU SEEN THESE COMPUTERIZED PETS the kids have been playing with lately? Most parents are thankful it's just a passing fad. And some wish it would pass a lot quicker. After all, you have to "feed" these little gizmos by punching the right buttons. You have to "walk" them at certain times. "Pet" them. "Clean up" after them. And doctor them. If you don't, they'll "die."

In a way, friendships are like that, aren't they? Friendships require maintenance. In fact, friendships are a lot like money: They're easier made than kept.

If you've ever had a friend who just drifted away, you know that. If you've ever watched a relationship fizzle, you've learned this the hard way. All of us, at one time or another, experience difficulties in our friendships. And these days, with the average American family moving to a new home every five years, things aren't getting any easier on the friendship front.

Over the last few months, I can't count how many people have told me that friendships have made their lives rich. Yet many lament the fact that they wish those friendships were better.

So how do we keep our friendships growing?

How can we be a better friend?

When UCLA football coach Pepper Rogers was in the middle of a disastrous season, he lamented to his wife that he had no friends. "My dog was my only friend," he recalls. "I told my wife that a man needs at least two friends, and she bought me another dog."

Perhaps Pepper, along with millions of others, could benefit from the following secrets to great friendships.

1. Accept others. On the way home from church, my four-year-old son sat in the backseat singing, "It's not my mama or my papa but it's me, O Lord, standing in the need of praise." He had the words a little mixed up, but he hit the truth right on the head. We all need to be encouraged, built up, and accepted by others. Good friends know that. Good friends accept people the way they are. They appreciate and praise the uniqueness of others. And they allow their friends the freedom to be themselves.

2. Listen up. After attending hundreds of formal receptions, Franklin D. Roosevelt decided to find out if anybody was really listening to him while he stood in the reception line. And so one night, as people came up to him with hands extended, he flashed his famous smile and said quietly, "I murdered my grandmother this morning." Guests would automatically respond with comments such as "How lovely!" or "Just continue with your great work, Mr. President." Nobody listened to what he was saying. Except for one foreign diplomat. When the president said, "I murdered my grandmother this morning," the diplomat responded softly, "I'm sure she had it coming."

No matter who we are, we all are looking for a listening ear. A friend of mine who was voted most popular girl in her entire high school once told me the secret to her popularity. Simply this: "I listen." From an early age her father had taught her that "everyone on earth is at least just a little bit lonely." I love that advice. An old Spanish proverb says, "Two great talkers will not travel far together." How true.

There is no better friendship booster than the ability to listen. The ability to show genuine interest in others is an admirable quality of a true friend.

3. Keep secrets. As a boy, I remember hearing the Jewish folktale of a man who went through a small community slandering the rabbi. One day, feeling suddenly remorseful, he begged the rabbi's forgiveness and offered to undergo any form of penance the rabbi thought suitable. "Go home," the rabbi told him, "find a feather pillow, cut it open, and scatter the feathers to the wind." Quickly the man did so and returned to the rabbi. "Am I now forgiven?" he asked. "Almost," came the reply, "just as soon as you gather all the feathers."

Scripture compares our words to arrows, because once an arrow is shot, it's tough to find and bring it back. In my experience, nothing destroys more friendships than the arrow of gossip. Many people live by the rule, "If you haven't got anything nice to say about anybody, come sit next to me." But when we gossip we violate Jesus' commandment: "Do unto others as you would have them do unto you." Proverbs 20:19 says, "A gossip betrays a confidence; so avoid a man who talks too much." Real friends speak well of you behind your back. They are known as people who won't receive gossip, nor will they pass it on. Remember: A closed mouth gathers no foot! Good friends aren't just there to listen to our secrets; they keep them.

4. Sharpen up. Proverbs 27:17 tells us that we are to sharpen each other "as iron sharpens iron."

Years ago a good friend of mine took me out for coffee one evening. "Phil," he said, as we ate pie together, "it's not fun for me to tell you this, but since we talked the other night I've felt I needed to confront you about something." I set my fork down and listened up. "Sometimes you have a real problem with gossip. And it's not helping anyone, least of all you." I didn't say much, but sat eating my pie. I hated to show my anger, but I was offended. How dare he talk to me like this? Who did he think he was? But the more I thought about it, the more I realized that he was right. Today, though we are many miles apart, I consider him to be one of my best friends.

"Wounds from a friend can be trusted" (Proverbs 27:6) because our best friends stab us in the front. It's true. Those who provoke change in us do so because they care enough to tell us the painful truth about ourselves. And mix it with a generous dose of love.

5. Practice forgiveness. When a friend who works in an office near mine came to work one morning, he found a can of Coke on his desk. On the side was a Post-It note bearing these words: "Sorry. I was a jerk. Can you ever forgive me?" Smiling, he walked down the hall with a message of forgiveness. You may have already guessed. The writer of the note was me. And later that day my friend brought me a can of Pepsi.

It is impossible for me to overstate the importance of forgiveness in friendship. Whether we are the one who hurts or the one who did the hurting, good friends humble themselves enough to admit when they are wrong. And good friends forgive. In fact, the gift of forgiveness is often the best gift we can offer a friend. And if it is accompanied by a can of Pepsi, so much the better.

6. Focus upward. There's an old Turkish proverb that goes like this: "He who seeks a faultless friend is friendless." How true. Friends fail us, don't they? People disappoint. And when we expect too much from our earthly friendships, we damage them. Realizing that the very best friends on earth will disappoint us takes the pressure off our friendships and strengthens them. God does not promise that *people* will never leave us nor forsake us. He promises that *He* will never leave. Ironically, those who seek lasting joy only in human relationships will end up lonely. The true joy of our lives will come from the most important relationship of all: our relationship with God. In loving Him, we learn to love our earthly friends better.

7. Be there. There's nothing like sickness or bankruptcy to help us discover who our real friends are.

During my wife's illness, her friend Julie informed us that she would be baby-sitting our three kids each Wednesday afternoon. Ramona had no choice in the matter. And so each Wednesday, Julie would show up and "kidnap" the kids, much to my wife's delight. To this day, Ramona often comments about Julie's kindness. Proverbs 17:17 says, "A friend loves at all times." When possible, be there when a friend needs you. If you can't be there, send a note or make a phone call. Perhaps the sweetest thing a friend could say about us is not that we were perfect or that we had all the answers. But that we were there.

Like houseplants, friendships grow slowly over time and require constant watering. Friendships that last a lifetime require nurturing, kindness, and a listening ear. Those who make such an investment find that it pays off all through the years.

Is there someone in your church, on your block, or in your office who needs your friendship? Are you willing to make the effort to reach out to them? I hope so. For I have found that life is richer, the horizon is brighter, and the road is shorter when traveled with a few good friends.

CHAPTER SEVENTEEN

Oprah and the Nearlywed Game

"I'd trade my fortune for just one happy marriage."
—BILLIONAIRE J. PAUL GETTY (1892–1976)

SINCE WRITING BOOKS ON THE TOPIC OF THE family, I often receive letters from readers seeking my advice. For instance, here's one from David LaMar of Plano, Texas. He writes, "Dear Mr. Callaway, who cuts your hair? Woodpeckers?"

Thankfully, Mr. LaMar wastes little time in moving on to his second paragraph: "I'm getting married this summer and I could use a little advice. Would you please write something about weddings?"

Now, please understand that I've never considered myself an expert. In fact, I have always made it clear that by the time I have it all together as a husband and a parent, I will either be deceased or unemployed. But that doesn't stop people from writing and phoning and e-mailing me with their questions. It's getting to the point where

Oprah could call any day, asking me to come on the show and field questions pertaining to marriage. When this happens, I imagine the scene will unfold something like this....

OPRAH (sitting comfortably on a satin sofa and smiling): "Phil, thanks for taking time out of your busy schedule to come to Chicago. Your book *What Wives Wish Their Husbands Knew About Yardwork* changed my life."

ME (nervously): "Thanks, Oprah, it's good to be here. Although ... I don't remember writing that book."

OPRAH (to audience): "See, I told you he'd be funny. Well, today in a segment called The Nearlywed Game, we will be bringing out a young man who is engaged to be married, and Phil will be offering him some expert advice. Will you welcome, please, David LaMar of Plano, Texas?"

DAVID (after sitting on the sofa beside Oprah): "Well, first of all, I need to apologize to Phil for a letter I wrote him some time ago. I asked if woodpeckers cut his hair."

OPRAH (looking at my hair): "Do they?"

ME: "I'd really rather talk about David."

OPRAH: Yes, you're right. This isn't the Jerry Springer Show. Now, David, you will be getting married later this year. Do you have some questions for our expert?"

DAVID: "Yes. First off, I'm wondering how much the wedding will cost me?"

ME: "Did you ever wonder why parents cry at weddings, David? According to the latest statistics, the average wedding costs a lot more than you will ever make. And that's just the wedding. Marriage and children will follow. It's like hockey superstar Bobby Hull said, 'My wife made me a millionaire. I used to have three million.'"

DAVID: "Who should we invite to the wedding?"

ME: "Your closest relatives. Your mother. Your father. Some brothers and sisters. A rich uncle. A rich aunt."

DAVID: "What about my potential mother-in-law?"

ME: "You should invite her, too."

DAVID: "No, no. What if *she* wants to invite more people?"

ME: "This is very important, David. From the start she must respect your ability to take charge. Yes, for too long we guys have sat in the back pew, unwilling to take the upper hand in such matters. For too long we have neglected to make the tough decisions. David, whatever you do, LISTEN TO HER."

DAVID: "What else should I know before I take the plunge?"

ME: "Realize that your wife will irritate you."

DAVID: "Pardon me?"

ME: "When we were dating, one of the things I admired most about Ramona was how slowly she moved. I was always in a hurry. She wasn't. I ran through the flower beds. She stopped to smell the petunias. I viewed this as a great virtue when I walked her to school in the morning and we didn't arrive until lunch, but now, on Sunday mornings, while I'm waiting in the car resisting the urge to honk, it can DRIVE ME NUTS!"

OPRAH (standing in audience now, holding mike in front of balding gentleman): "Phil, it sounds like you could use a little advice yourself."

ME: "We all could, Oprah. We all could."

BALDING GENTLEMAN: "Phil, what are the characteristics of a great marriage?"

ME: "A deaf husband and a blind wife."

BALDING GENTLEMAN: "No, seriously, I'm getting married soon, too. What can I do to make my marriage last?"

ME: "Leave no alternatives."

BALDING GENTLEMAN: "What do you mean?"

ME: "If you're getting married with anything less than *staying* married in mind, it's the wrong step. Marriage is a lifelong commitment. No matter what comes your way, you will stay faithful to your promise. I've been married now for 15 years and I can say that few things equal the joy of sitting across the table from your wife and saying, 'Honey, this tomato soup tastes like cardboard, but I love you more every day.'"

OPRAH (fighting back tears): "Phil, that was so touching. Is there anything else?"

ME: "Yes, Oprah. Marry the one you love, then love the one you marry."

BALDING GENTLEMAN: "Is there more?"

ME: "Yes, much more. Try praising your wife. She'll love you for it. Once she gets over the initial shock."

DAVID: "I want to have a great marriage. Where's the best place to start?"

ME: "Keep the lines of communication open at all costs. It's the key to a great marriage."

DAVID: "Sorry, could you repeat that? I was thinking of something else."

ME: "That's something you'll have to work on, David. Marriage will pay great dividends. If you pay interest."

DAVID: "What are some practical ways to make a marriage better?"

ME: "Try harder to keep your wife than you did to get her. Love her. Respect her. Romance her. Be forgiving. Be gentle. Pray together. Read the Bible together. And use the laundry hamper."

OPRAH: "Phil, has your own marriage been perfect?"

ME: "Well, I have a confession to make. I married the wrong woman. At least that's what an older man told me a week before Ramona and I walked the aisle. And maybe he was right. She could have done a lot better. But while our incompatibilities made for some tough times, God brought us through them. Imperfect people won't have perfect marriages. But those who walk with God learn to walk together."

OPRAH (no longer holding back the tears): "Phil, this has been so good. So practical. I wish we could go on, but we're out of time and I'm out of Kleenex. Do you have one more question, David?"

DAVID: "Yes. I'd like to invite Phil to our wedding. It's on August 30."

ME: "I'd love to come, David. But that's woodpecker season where I live. And I'm scheduled for a haircut."

OPRAH: "Join us tomorrow, when we'll be discussing James Dobson's new book, *Making Life Rich Without Any Money.*"

CHAPTER EIGHTEEN

The First C to a Successful Marriage

"Success in marriage is more than finding the right person: it is being the right person."

—ROBERT BROWNING (1812–1889)

IT IS MONDAY NIGHT. I'VE JUST TUCKED IN THE kids, picked up another soft drink, and settled down on the couch. My favorite team is three points behind the Dallas Cowboys. My favorite wife is seated nearby, reading *Women Are from Cleveland, Men Are from the Bronx*.

Suddenly the cordless phone rings.

Picking it up, I listen for a full 15 minutes, saying only "uh-huh," then hang up, not once taking my eyes off the television set.

"Who was that?" asks Ramona from behind the book.

"Oh, just Biff Slootweg."

"Well?" she says.

"Well what?"

"Well . . . we haven't seen Biff since 1976. How is he?"

"Fine," I say.

"Fine? What did he say?"

"He said he's fine."

"Come on. What *else* did he say?" Ramona sets the book aside, a sure sign that I am about to be subjected to relentless district-attorney-type questions that will not let up even after the two-minute warning. So pushing the "Mute" button, I tell her the truth.

The truth is that Biff is fine. Ever since the discovery that his adoptive parents weren't really Russian spies after all, but were working for Iraq, Biff started skipping school and began sneaking around the world with them, keeping the CIA informed of their every move. Then came that fateful night aboard the nuclear submarine when they discovered the tiny microchips he had implanted in their earlobes, and Biff was tossed into a Baghdad prison where he was flogged daily until his dramatic escape in a blimp during the Gulf War.

"Wow!" says Ramona. "That's amazing."

"See," I say, punching the "Mute" button, "I told you he was fine."

If the previous conversation has the slightest ring of familiarity to it, chances are that you suffer from Communication Deficit Disorder, too. Please understand that you are not alone. I, together with millions of others, feel your pain.

After 25 years of a less-than-blissful marriage, a husband and wife finally agreed to see a counselor. Five minutes into their first session, the counselor turned to the husband and asked, "What would you say has been the biggest problem in your marriage?"

Fidgeting in his chair, the husband replied, "My wife's a lousy communicator. We can't even carry on an intelligent conversation and I want to divorce her."

"Do you have any grounds?" asked the counselor.

"Oh yes, we do," replied the husband. "In fact, we have 13 acres."

"No, no," said the counselor. "I mean . . . well . . . do you have a grudge?"

The husband shook his head, "No," he replied, "but we do have a carport."

Communication. Most of us understand how important it is, but few of us are adept at it. I must admit that my communication skills leave much to be desired. And they are at their lowest point when my wife stands before me and asks, "Do you think I'm fat?"

The thing about this question is that there is no correct answer. If you say "no" it means "yes." "Yes" means "yes." "Sort of" means "absolutely." If you laugh during any of your answers, you could go without a well-balanced meal for weeks.

———

During the years since Biff called, I would like to think I've shown some improvement in the communication area. In fact, here are three things I've learned that, for the most part, have brought harmony, static-free communication lines, and some well-balanced meals into our home.

1. Men and women are different. It's not rocket science, but men and women have different expectations, different aspirations, different needs. For instance, my wife needs nurturing, friendship, protection, romance, faithfulness, and clothes that fit, whereas I need food, sex, and . . . well . . . I can't think of anything else offhand. I may be exaggerating here, but the point is, we are very different. I have found that when we celebrate our differences, when I put my wife's needs ahead of my own and view my own selfishness more seriously than any faults she may display, we draw closer together.

2. Forgetfulness can be a virtue. Last Christmas, after a petty argument, my wife and I did not speak to each other for a full three days. This gave "Silent Night" a whole new meaning for us. The reason for our disagreement was so petty that two days into my vow of silence, I couldn't remember what started it. But when Ramona began sneaking my presents out from under the tree and returning them to fine hardware stores everywhere, the thought hit me: *You know, at one point this wasn't such a big deal.* Then I remembered Ephesians 4:32: "Be kind and compassionate to one another, forgiving each other, just as in Christ God forgave you." *God is in the business of forgiving and forgetting,* I thought. *I'd better be, too.*

"Honey," I said, with great difficulty, "I'm sorry. I was wrong." As it turned out, she was quick to forgive.

She even brought back the presents.

3. Use your ears more than your mouth. Or as Shakespeare put it: "Give every man thine ear, but few thy voice." In our marriages, in our friendships, in our relationship with God, we must master the art of listening. I readily admit that I have a long way to go in this area. "Knowing when to say nothing is 50 percent of tact and

90 percent of marriage," wrote Sydney Harris, and the apostle James agreed: "Everyone should be quick to listen, slow to speak and slow to become angry" (James 1:19).

Without exception, the best times I've spent with my wife always come along when I listen. When I put her first. When I hit my own "Mute" button and show genuine interest in her world.

Now, I'd better go. The phone's ringing and it may be Biff. On second thought, perhaps I'll let my wife answer.

CHAPTER NINETEEN

The Power of Commitment

"My most brilliant achievement was my ability to persuade my wife to marry me."

—WINSTON CHURCHILL (1874–1965)

THE GREAT PHILOSOPHER SOCRATES ONCE WROTE, "By all means, marry. If you get a good wife, you will become very happy. If you get a bad one, you'll become a philosopher."

Some time ago, my parents were visiting and I asked them about the secret to their 55-year marriage. Without hesitation, Dad said, "Senility. I wake up each morning and I can't remember who this old girl is. So each day is a new adventure." When Mom finally quit pinching him, he got serious.

"In a word?" he said. "Commitment."

You don't have to stand in the checkout line long to know that commitment is not a hallmark of our culture. Standing near the chocolate bars the other day, I picked out a tabloid and read of Rex and Teresa LeGalley, a young couple who want to ensure that their recent marriage will stand the test of time. After all, it was Teresa's second marriage and Rex's third. So they drew up a 16-page prenuptial agreement that specifies such details as what time they'll go to bed, how often they'll have sex, which gasoline they'll purchase, and who will do the laundry. Says Teresa, "This is the plan that we think will keep us married for 50 or 60 years."[8]

When I told this to Dad, he had another one-word response: "Ha!"

Occasionally Hollywood surprises us with some good news, though. Famed singer and actress Bette Midler, who has been married for 13 years to artist Martin von Haselberg, was asked about the key to their marriage. Midler responded, "Separate vacations." Then, like my dad, she got serious. "We're committed," she said. "We're in it for the long haul. Besides, you really don't get to know a person until you've known them a long time, and we don't know each other yet, even though it's been 13 years. Sometimes it's been a struggle, but amazingly we didn't give up."[9]

Mel Gibson, who was married the same year as Midler, agrees. Recently the popular movie star found himself talking with an older man about marriage. "We were having a real heart-to-heart," recalls Gibson, "then his wife appeared. She was a beautiful girl about 19 or 20. And I said, 'Oh, you are a lucky man.' " The man shook his head and answered, "I should have stayed with my first wife. Things haven't changed—she just looks different." Gibson sums it up, "You see, people are chasing things they can't get. They're just illusions. You've got to make a commitment in marriage—just say, 'This is it.' I think too many people go into marriage too lightly. You've got to take it seriously—go in there to make it last."[10]

When asked by *US* magazine about the secret to his 41-year marriage, James Garner, the star of *Maverick* and *The Rockford Files,* said, "Consideration. You have to care for [your spouse] and do a lot of forgiving and forgetting. It's a two-way street. A lot of people don't get married because they know they can get out of it at any minute. Hey, it was difficult for me to make that commitment, but when I make them, I stick with them."

I remember reading of an elderly couple whose family had thrown a golden anniversary party for them. The husband was deeply touched by their kindness and stood to thank them. Then he looked at his wife of 50 years and tried to put into words just how he felt about her. Lifting his glass he said: "My dear wife, after 50 years I've found you tried and true." Everyone smiled their approval, but not his wife. She had hearing trouble, so she cupped one hand behind an ear and said, "Eh?" Her husband repeated himself loudly, "AFTER FIFTY YEARS I'VE FOUND YOU TRIED AND TRUE!" His wife shot back, "Well, let me tell YOU something—after 50 years I'm tired of you, too!"

Thankfully, commitment doesn't need to be like that. Marriage is not a life sentence; it is a joyful privilege. Paul Brand, the missionary doctor who worked for many years among leprosy victims in India, said these challenging words: "As I enter my sixth decade of marriage I can say without a flicker of hesitation that the basic human virtue of faithfulness to one partner is the most joyful way of life. . . . I have always trusted my wife completely, and she me.

We have each been able to channel love and commitment and intimacy to one person—a lifelong investment that is now, in old age, paying rich dividends."[11]

A friend once told me that his parents always got along. That he had never heard them disagree, and he had certainly never heard them argue. I finally stopped laughing long enough to tell him that I couldn't say that about Mom and Dad. But I never doubted their commitment to each other. What kept them committed? Simple obedience to the One with whom they had the most important relationship of all.

———

Often at night, I came into Mom and Dad's room and found them praying together. Or reading the Bible together. They knew that "unless the LORD builds the house, its builders labor in vain" (Psalm 127:1). Mom told me one day, "Only with Christ at the center of our marriage, at the center of our home, at the center of everything we do, can we experience the greatest joy and fulfillment possible."

My wife and I have made a commitment to read the Bible and pray together before we go to sleep each night. We haven't always achieved that goal. In fact, sometimes we have gone through weeks of neglecting it altogether. But when we follow through on this simple commitment, it can make a world of difference in our marriage. For one thing, I find it very difficult to read passages like Colossians 3:12-14 aloud to my wife without it having a dramatic effect on the way I treat her:

> Clothe yourselves with compassion, kindness, humility, gentleness and patience. Bear with each other and forgive

whatever grievances you may have against one another. Forgive as the Lord forgave you. And over all these virtues put on love, which binds them all together in perfect unity.

It is Christ alone who gives us the power to love others in this way.

Believe me, ours is not a perfect marriage. But I am far richer when I remember the three "Cs" of a great marriage: Communication. Commitment. Christ.

It may not be the deepest thing you'll ever read, but I'd rather be a happily married man than a philosopher. Any day.

CHAPTER TWENTY

The Incredible Worth
of a Memory

"Together we stick; divided we're stuck."
—EVON HEDLEY

ON FEBRUARY 25, 1996, HAING NGOR, WHO survived the horrors of the Khmer Rouge in Cambodia and gave an Oscar-winning performance in *The Killing Fields,* was murdered in Los Angeles. At first there was speculation that he had been killed for political reasons linked to the film, but recently the truth came out. When Ngor escaped to Thailand and arrived in America, he had only one possession: a photograph of his precious wife, who was killed while a captive. Ngor had the photo mounted in a gold locket and wore it faithfully about his neck. When a street gang held him at gunpoint, Ngor gave them his 9,600-dollar Rolex watch, but refused to surrender the gold locket.

"Ultimately," said the prosecuting attorney, "this photo, which meant more to Dr. Ngor than life itself, is the reason why he died."[12]

When I heard this tragic story, I thought of the people who mean the most to me. What could be more precious than their memory?

Most of us, when asked to gauge the richness of our lives, think immediately of people. Those who have cried with us, laughed with us, and shaped who we are. Here are the memories of some homemakers, pastors, and authors who have discovered the richness of relationships and wouldn't surrender them for all the world.

———

"For me there has been no greater joy or satisfaction than serving Christ by serving my family. We are seeing incredible dividends from the investment we have made in raising our kids. As long as we are alive we'll be celebrating the fact that our three children are deeply in love with Jesus. A Relationship Invested in a Christ-centered Home spells RICH to me."

———

"The thing that's made my life rich is the same thing that's kept me most without money: my children (we just had number 7). With kids you experience the full range of emotions. Joy, elation, sadness, anger, happiness, sorrow, laughter, tears. You name it, kids will help you experience it. I wouldn't trade a minute with my kids for anything life could have given me without them."

———

"I am rich because I just had the joy of leading my son-in-law to faith in Christ."

———

"My best memories are of family sports, such as snow skiing, being pulled on a raft behind a boat, playing golf, or just walking down a beach. Those times of just doing things together do so much to set the stage for more intimate moments between my wife and me and our two children. When my children were younger, I always insisted on taking them on errands with me because I never knew what would happen next. I loved making a game out of those errands. In a nutshell, it's been time, not money, that has made life rich for me."

———

"I think I got my crow's-feet as a result of so much time up close and personal with my friends. They know how to help me smile and see the humorous side of life. At the best of times, they seem to understand my past, believe in my future, and accept me just as I am today."

———

"Recently I became a charter member of a secret society we call The Barnabas Group. It consists of three friends in our office complex who watch for opportunities to encourage other members of our staff. We send an attractive little box with a note, a card, or a few sticks of gum, and tell them how much they are appreciated. What a difference this makes around the office. Sometimes we even give ourselves a box so other members of the staff won't get suspicious."

"I am rich in memories. Memories of when our children were small. Going on family skiing trips, vacations, birthdays. I am rich in friends. The supportive kind. Yesterday I sat in a restaurant with a friend chatting for three hours. I was seriously ill this past fall—and when I was in the hospital I was showered with flowers and cards. How rich I felt!"

"When a friend of mine moved across the country to a new job, the last thing he did was borrow 50 dollars from me. I told him I would lend it on one condition, that he repay it by sending me five letters with 10 dollars in each. Over the next year, he wrote every few months with updates about his job and his family and his new life. Each of his five letters contained ten dollars. When the last installment arrived, I sent him a letter. It included a check for 50 dollars."

"My husband and I were talking with another couple whose home burned to the ground last summer. The fire started late at night and their two young children were asleep. While his wife carried the kids from the house, the father pulled out the most important things he could think of. He ran past the TV set, the VCR, even his wallet, and chose instead their entire collection of photo albums and home videotapes. His wife keeps telling him what a wise choice he made."

"I am a widowed grandfather who used to think Santa Claus had the right idea: Visit people only once a year. But as I near 70 and my health isn't what it used to be, I'm increasingly aware of the importance of the people God puts into our lives. The only time I move quickly anymore is when I pull my grandkids' pictures out of my wallet. They are the best-looking, smartest kids in the world. My children ask me to visit several times a year now. They know what I'll do. I'll visit them, spoil their kids, then go home smiling."

Part IV

RICH PEOPLE
KNOW WHERE
THE BUCK STOPS

Winston Churchill believed that when it comes to money, people can be divided into three categories: "Those who are billed to death, those who are worried to death, and those who are bored to death."

I suppose I fit neatly into the first category. We were so poor that at one point my only possession was a hand-me-down toothbrush. But when life doesn't make cents, we can still make it rich. And when we're born with a silver spoon in our mouths, we can melt it down and turn it into something useful. The apostle Paul said, "I have learned in whatever state I am to be content."

In the coming chapters you will meet a cheapskate, a billionaire, and an infamous televangelist. All three are learning a great irony: Those who set their minds and hearts on money are equally disappointed whether they get it or not.

CHAPTER TWENTY-ONE

Our Money Pit

"The wages of spend is debt."
—MARK HEARD (1951–1992)

IF YOU'RE LIKE MOST NORTH AMERICANS MY age, at some point—usually after about six extra-strength Tylenol—you have considered building a house. In my case, the idea hit me back in 1984 when I had a temperature of 103, but not until a year ago did I muster up the courage to tell my wife. "Honey," I said one evening, "how about we . . . um . . . how about I pour you a cup of hot herbal tea and rub your back?"

She said, "What do you want, Phil?"

I said, "Sweetie, I love you so much, you're like ice cream on my pie. How about we build a house?"

"WHAT?" she exclaimed rather loudly. "We don't have any money."

She had a good point there, so I had to think quickly.

"The bank does," I countered.

"You can't rob a bank, Phil. Remember? You're in ministry."

"We'll take out a mortgage," I suggested. "Remember the movie *It's a Wonderful Life*? Bankers are like Jimmy Stewart. They exist to help others."

"How much help will we need?" she asked.

"Um," I replied, drawing on some of the accounting skills I'd acquired back in high school, "I think it will cost quite a bit. But we've been renting now for 15 years, and I figure we've spent 81,000 dollars at it. This way, instead of putting the 81,000 dollars into rent, we can put it into taxes, utilities, interest, and repairs."

For some reason she wasn't sold yet.

"Look," I continued, "it's not like we'll go over budget or anything. We'll just count the cost, then begin. After all, how much trouble can wood, hay, and siding be?"

"But there are thousands of decisions to be made," Ramona reminded me. "We're both the youngest in our families, and youngest kids have difficulty making decisions, don't they?"

"I'm not sure. I don't think so. What do you think?"

"I'm not sure either."

On the morning of June 12, the excavation began. At noon the contractor called on his fuzzy cellular. "We have a slight problem, Phil," he said, which is a bit like the Titanic's navigator warning the captain of ice cubes ahead. "We've hit a pit. A BIG pit."

"Um . . . ," I gulped, ". . . why don't you just fill it in?"

"It's not that simple," he hollered. "It's got WATER in it. LOTS of water. You have a SPRING!"

"How deep is the pit?" I yelled, as his cellular began to fade. "Well," I think I heard him say, "there are Chinese children swimming in it."

That night, I didn't sleep much for the nightmares. In my dream, our house was an exact replica of the Titanic. As we sat around the dining-room table, calmly eating our exotic dinner, the ship began tilting to starboard. Fine china plates slid across the table and water began pouring in the windows. Outside, neighbors rowed by with no room in their lifeboats, holding their hands over their hearts. The last sound they heard as we sank slowly out of sight was the eerie lullaby my wife sang to comfort us: "My debt will go on."

I awoke in a cold sweat. "A man's home is his hassle," I said out loud. Ramona stirred beside me. "Chicken soup," she said incoherently, then awoke and asked me what was wrong. "The pit," I said. "Do you have any idea how much it will cost to build a solid foundation now?"

"We could sell bottled water," she offered. "Callaway Springs. We'll start a rumor about seeing the pope's reflection in it. People will come from everywhere."

"The water's green," I said. "It tastes like Roundup."

She patted my chest. "It's just money, Honey. We can do without some things. Furniture. Windows. Heat." Then she reminded me of a sermon I'd just preached. A sermon on trust. "You think God doesn't know about this?" she asked. "It'll be fine." Then we prayed together. And I rolled over and slept like a baby. A baby with colic.

Today, after five months and six ulcers, we are a SITCOM family. A Single Income Three Children Oppressive Mortgage family. We also have a different address. And a new view. Sometimes I find myself saying things I never thought I'd say. Things like: "Hey! You kids clean that lipstick off the wall RIGHT NOW!" or,

"Jeffrey, if I catch you pounding nails into that oak door again I'll call the police!"

"It's just a house," my wife reminds me three times a day. And I'm starting to listen. Thankfully, it's a house with the most solid foundation in town. An engineer spent a good hour sampling our soil for proof. "It's unsinkable," he smiled, dropping a 600-dollar invoice into my hands. And I thought again of the Titanic.

Last night I went to bed exhausted, only to have my daughter, Rachael, crawl in beside me. "Daddy," she said, folding her hands behind her head and gazing at the freshly painted ceiling, "I like the old house better."

"Why?" I asked sleepily.

"I just like it," she said. "You don't read to us here. You've been sorta cranky." And I was wide awake.

We had a family powwow then. We talked about taking care of the stuff God gives us. About giving it all back to Him. Then we prayed together. "Dear God," I said, "I've been so busy building a house that I've forgotten to build a home. Please forgive me." My wife thanked God for new things. For new houses. For new starts. After reading to the kids, I went to bed. And slept like a baby. Without any colic at all.

————

By the way, the other night a friend asked me what one feature in our new house I enjoy the most. I thought for a minute, then told him about my bathtub. You see, I spent an extra 175 dollars on a tub that is larger than normal and has jets that shoot water at you. It is physically possible for you to enter one of these a grape and come out a raisin.

Sometimes at night I enjoy relaxing in the tub and reading a favorite book. Occasionally I catch myself dreaming of what I would do differently if I were crazy enough to build again, but then I realize how silly that is and I start thanking God for what He has given me. For a house that's still afloat. A family that's still intact. And a tub that's just my size.

Now, if only I had enough money to put water in it.

CHAPTER TWENTY-TWO

The Trouble with Cheapskates

"Misers aren't much fun to live with. But they make wonderful ancestors."

—TERRY GLASPEY

FOR AS LONG AS I CAN REMEMBER, I'VE BEEN A cheapskate. Just ask Willie Major, a former friend of mine. When Willie was five and I was old enough to know better, we "borrowed" his mother's change purse and set off in search of a candy store. Knowing that I was older and wiser and could be trusted completely, Willie put me in charge of the purse strings. On the way to the store, I untied those purse strings and offered Willy some free advice:

"The brown ones are best," I informed him, as the pennies slid slowly between my fingers. "You really wanna hold onto these babies. But see these silver ones? These are no good. You don't want 'em, Willie. You give these to someone else. Someone like me."

(Note: Willie has now changed his name to Will and become a lawyer. If you're reading this, Will, allow me to say that I was wrong and I certainly hope things are going very well for you. I hope that you have plenty of suspects to prosecute without thinking of your dear old friend. P.S.: I NEVER laugh at lawyer jokes. No, sir. Not me.)

Thirty years have passed and I trust my ethics have improved. But I must admit, I'm still as cheap as a second-hand chewing gum.

A few summers ago, due to the generosity of our publishing house, Ramona and I piled three kids into our rusting Ford and drove down the coast of Oregon to spend five days in a condo overlooking the Pacific Ocean. It was a cheapskate's dream vacation: free maid service, free parking, even a McDonald's nearby.

Now you must understand that although I'm cheap, I have a deep appreciation of the luxuries others have paid for. In fact, my idea of roughing it is setting the air conditioner on low in the RV. Of course, there's a slight problem. We do not have an RV. We do not even have a tent that fits. So on the three-day trip to this gorgeous getaway, the five of us camped in the only thing we could afford: a tent which slept three of us comfortably. Now, we've always been a close-knit family, but this was pushing it. Crammed into four sleeping bags, the rain pounding inches from our noses, and me too cheap to buy air mattresses, we groaned in agony as I told stories of the good old days, back when men were men and their wives were tired of it.

"Kids, did I ever tell you about the time wolves carried away my mother-in-law?" I asked, before being pushed out the tent flap by my dear wife, whose sense of humor had vanished at the stroke of midnight. "On second thought, perhaps it was your Uncle Ivan," I yelled from outside the tent, then stood up, whacking my head on a tree branch.

The next morning as I drove along at 55, nursing a welt which bore a startling resemblance to Mount Saint Helens, my wife reached over and gently patted my knee. "Honey," she said, in a voice that warned of things to come, "you are the cheapest person I have ever been married to."

"Wait a minute," I said. "That's not fair. I know cheaper people. For example, there's um . . . there's—" One hundred miles later, I still couldn't think of anyone. "I'm not all that bad" was all I could say.

"Oh yes, you are, Phil," said Ramona, "and right now you will pull over to that Wal-Mart where we will buy air mattresses, or tonight we'll see what the wolves do with you!"

"Honey," I asked, "is something troubling you?"

That night, as the children snored comfortably on their $19.95 air mattresses, Ramona and I argued about the trouble with cheapskates. "Are we in debt?" I asked defensively. "Have we been spending money before making it?"

"No," replied Ramona, "but are we balanced? Are we generous? Are we holding things loosely?"

I pretended to be asleep.

"Phil," she said, "you're so cheap you bought air mattresses for everyone but yourself."

"If I promise to quit being so cheap," I said, "will you let me share yours?"

"Okay," she laughed. And she did.

As you can tell, one of Ramona's virtues is patience (something I continue to help her practice). On this, the cheapest trip we ever took, our disagreements centered solely on money. And, though it pains me to admit it, I was usually wrong.

During early-morning walks along an Oregon beach I began to realize this. Each morning as the sun rose, I read a chapter from the book of Matthew, then walked a few miles thinking about it. But mostly, I must admit, I thought about the condo, and longed for a little more luxury in my life. After reading Matthew 6 one morning, I noticed Jesus' command, "You cannot serve both God and Money." *Obviously a command for the wealthy,* I thought, as I walked down the beach, mentally calculating the gas mileage we'd been getting on the trip.

Then it hit me harder than that tree branch: Jesus wasn't just talking to the wealthy. He was talking to people like me. You see, even a penny, if held close enough to the eye, can block our view of Him. It doesn't have to be much, but if it's where I fix my eyes, I will miss the most important thing. "Lord," I prayed, "help me to be content wherever I am. Help me to hold the stuff of earth loosely, and worship only You."

As the rain began to fall on the last night of our vacation, we crammed once again into the tent. When the kids finally grew quiet, I asked them, "What did you like most about this trip?" Was it the condo? The sand castles? The ocean? Their answer took me by surprise. All three agreed: It was camping in a three-man tent.

"Dad, tell us about the wolf and Gramma," asked one of them.

"You wouldn't," warned my wife.

And I didn't.

I may be slow. But it doesn't take a whack on the head to wake me up. Then again, maybe it does.

CHAPTER TWENTY-THREE

The Only Guaranteed Investment

"The stuff of earth competes for allegiance I owe only to the Giver of all good things"

—RICH MULLINS (1955–1997)

YEARS AGO, WHEN MUHAMMAD ALI RULED THE boxing world, he was stopped for speeding on his way to a title fight. When the police officer pulled him over and informed Ali's limousine driver that the ticket would cost them 100 dollars, the famous boxer handed his driver 200 dollars.

"Give this to him," he commanded.

"And tell him we're coming back this way."

There's no doubt about it, money has its advantages. Of course, it won't buy you happiness, it won't buy you love, and it certainly won't buy what it used to, but I'd be foolish to say that money won't buy anything. As Lord Mancroft said, "Money, if it does not bring you happiness,

will at least help you to be miserable in comfort." Here are
a few of the things money can—and cannot—buy:

> Nice houses, but not a home.
> A fancy bed, but not a peaceful sleep.
> Companions, but not friends.
> Food, but not satisfaction.
> Sex, but not love.
> New cars, but not safety.
> Pills, but not health.
> Fun, but not fulfillment.
> Sun-filled vacations, but not peace.

Just yesterday *The Telegraph* in London reported that
during a night of excess, an unnamed pop-star couple
spent 1200 dollars filling their hotel bath with three cases
of Mumm champagne. While they were downstairs eating dinner in the posh Portobello Hotel restaurant, however, a maid arrived to clean their room. Noticing that the
bathtub was full, she did what she'd been trained to do:
She pulled the plug on the tiny bubbles. Fortunately for
her, the couple managed to laugh off the incident. "When
you earn over 32 million dollars a year it does not really
matter, does it?" the hotel manager told reporters. "They
saw the funny side."

Reading this story, I was reminded of the times I have,
to a lesser degree, pulled the plug on some great "ground-
level" opportunity. We've all got our stories. A friend of
mine sometimes laments the fact that his grandfather
owned major shares in IBM. Until he forgot where he hid
them. When I was a kid we had three shoe boxes full of
baseball cards. Many times I have wondered where Mom
put them. I'm sure those boxes were crammed full of

Mickey Mantle and Babe Ruth rookie cards. Who knows what happened to them? Who knows who pulled the plug?

During frenzied stock-market trading recently, the five richest Americans saw the value of their principal holdings shrink by nearly 4 billion dollars in one day. Bill Gates, chief executive of Microsoft, lost 1.76 billion dollars. The Walton family, which owns Wal-Mart, lost 1.64 billion dollars. Of course, none of them will be coming soon to a soup line near you, but their losses should remind us that in this life there are few guarantees. Sometimes money talks. And sometimes it says good-bye.

On television and radio, in magazines and newspapers, get-rich-quick schemes abound. Telemarketing reps inform us that the future is ours with a few wise investments. In the last six months I have been approached on numerous occasions by people—many of them Christians—with dollar signs in their eyes. "Phil, this product has really changed our lives," they tell me. "We'd love to sign you up to sell it." Of course I have nothing against making a living, but I must admit that I'm alarmed at the trend among North American Christians to put so much stock in the temporary. In the latest product. The latest fad. Don't get me wrong. I support the wise handling of our finances. There is a time for retirement savings plans. But they will never secure our future.

Jesus had much to say about money (about one-fifth of His recorded words, in fact) because He knew of our propensity to fall in love with it. To worship it. To find our security in it. And so He challenged us to "store up for yourselves treasures in heaven, where moth and rust do not destroy, and where thieves do not break in and steal"

(Matthew 6:20). In 1 Peter 1:3,4, the apostle Peter talked about the only guaranteed and lasting investment: "In his great mercy he has given us new birth into a living hope through the resurrection of Jesus Christ from the dead, and into an inheritance that can never perish, spoil or fade—kept in heaven for you. . . ."

Our possessions are a trust from God. What we clutch tightly, we lose. What we place in His hands, we will possess. For eternity.

This lesson hasn't come easily for me. But it finally started to hit home during two adventures that literally changed my life. The first began one hot summer night in Georgia.

CHAPTER TWENTY-FOUR

The Beggar and the Billionaire

"With money in your pocket, you are wise, and you are handsome, and you sing well too."

—JEWISH PROVERB

FOR A CANADIAN KID LIKE ME, ATLANTA IS HOT in July. Like opening the oven door and poking your head in to see if the bread is done. As my plane touches down, I pack up a book I've been reading and step into the Georgia night.[13] A taxi driver talks of weather and baseball's Braves, but my mind is haunted by a question the book has raised: "If grace is so amazing, why don't Christians show more of it?"

It is midnight when I arrive at my hotel, anxious for a cool room. A smiling employee informs me that my "guaranteed room reservation" is no longer guaranteed. "But I phoned ahead twice to ensure my reservations," I tell her angrily. "I'm sorry," she says. "Some guests have stayed longer than expected. We're sending you to another hotel." Handing me 15 dollars for a taxi, she listens to my response. It is anything but grace-full.

The bill comes to ten dollars, and I pocket what's left. Small consolation for the fact that I am now in a darker area of town. Closing the curtains tight against beggars and bums, I push my luggage against the door and sit down to prepare for tomorrow's business—a grueling schedule which includes conducting a magazine interview with the first billionaire I've ever met.

Growing up, I somehow learned to view the wealthy with suspicion. After all, the love of money was the root of all kinds of evil, wasn't it? And who could love money more than the man with lots of it? I begin writing out questions for tomorrow's interview. They come fast: "Jesus said it was easier for a camel to squeeze through the eye of a needle than for a rich man to enter the kingdom of heaven. How come? And how does a billionaire live a rich life? I've always heard that rich people are miserable."

Outside on the darkened street, beggars look for an outstretched hand. As I drift off, I find myself wondering how I could get just a small handout from the billionaire.

After a few restless hours of sleep, I peek through the curtains. The streets are swept clean of beggars now, but the early-morning sun makes the shabby buildings seem darker than the night before. I can't help thinking of the contrast between where I am and where I'm going.

Breakfast is toast and juice and soon, under the watchful eye of his two assistants, I'm shaking hands with one of the wealthiest Christians on earth. A giant in the investment world, Robert Van Kampen is the pioneer of the insured mutual fund, and founder and financial backer of the *Scriptorium,* the world's largest private collection of biblical manuscripts. Today he manages six companies with investments of over 70 billion dollars, a figure I still can't fathom.

His opening remarks surprise me. "Don't be alarmed if I don't make it through this interview," he smiles, tapping a small heart-rate monitor. "I have to check this thing every few minutes now. Doctor's orders, you know." He tells me of his recurring health problems. "Some things money can't buy."

"What can it buy?" I ask him.

"Well, when your motive is right, when God is number one, you'd be surprised what money can do."

"Like what?"

"Ten years ago I was shown a sixteenth-century Bible whose owner was killed for possessing it. It still had his blood stains on it. This made such an impact on me that I bought the Bible and decided to commit myself to the collection and preservation of early manuscripts. The one thing I would die for is the preservation of God's truth. Money has helped me have a part in that."

"What would you say has made your life rich?"

He hesitates for a few moments. "Giving money away. I've found that you can never outgive God. If you give to get, chances are you won't get a dime. If you're giving out of a heart of gratitude for what God has given you, God turns around and blesses you. I've made some huge errors. I've lost more money in a year than some countries make. But the Lord makes it up to you if your motive is right. My life is a story of grace. I started with nothing and I've been incredibly successful. God has trusted me with these funds and He could take them away at any moment. To the best of my ability I want to be trustworthy with what He's given me. God rewards our faithfulness whether we have a little or a lot."

He stops to check the monitor. "How do Christians treat you?" I ask.

"It's funny," he says. "Nobody likes a successful businessman, especially if he's a Christian. The only people that like you are the ones you're giving money to. Most people who get to know me now have an agenda. That's why some of my best friends are people I knew before I was successful. They liked me then. They like me now. I get so many requests from people for money . . ."

"That's why I came to see you," I say, laughing a little too loudly.[14]

———————

That night as I arrive at my hotel, a homeless man calls out for my attention: "Hey, man, why you walk on by? Why you treat me like garbage?"

I stop. Perhaps unwisely.

"I'm sorry," I say. "I didn't mean to—" He holds out a free pass to "The Gentleman's Club," a nude show just down the street. I show him my wedding ring. "I'm a Christian," I say, "and it's tough enough on business trips without you tempting me, man." We laugh together. He can't stop apologizing. "I'm a Christian, too," he says, tossing a cigarette. "And . . . I'm ashamed."

A policeman stops and gets out of his car. "Everything alright?" he asks in a Southern drawl. I assure him that it is.

"They ain't used to no one talkin' to us," the beggar tells me, as the car pulls away.

For the next half hour I sit on the curb listening to his story. Loss of job. Loss of family. Drugs. Alcohol. Depression. Attempted suicide. "Last night I slept behind them garbage cans," he points, his breath causing me to inch away. "A rat bit me in the knuckle . . . right here."

Not knowing what to believe, I ask him, "So what would Jesus say to you?"

"Oh, man . . . He'd say that He loves me. I sit over by them garbage cans most nights and I don't sing so hot, but I sing 'Amazing grace! How sweet the sound! That saved a wretch like me! . . .' God's grace. It's the only thing that's got me through."

The police car coasts slowly by and I sit quietly, reflecting on his words. Reflecting on my tendency to judge too quickly.

Then I pull the five dollars from my pocket and add a few more. "I don't know how you'll spend this," I say, "but that's not up to me."

After teaching me a series of handshakes, he listens as I urge him to try to get his job back. Then we part ways. Sometimes his words still echo in my ears: "God's grace. It's the only thing that's got me through."

CHAPTER TWENTY-FIVE

Me and Jim Bakker

"There, but for the grace of God, goes John Bradford."
—JOHN BRADFORD (1510-1555)

WHEN I WAS INFORMED BY A NASHVILLE publicist that Jim Bakker would like to talk with me, I must admit that I wasn't impressed. The sad truth is, I didn't much like the disgraced televangelist. A few years back you couldn't stand at a checkout counter or flip on a TV set without sharing in his disgrace. I'd even found myself laughing at jokes about his wife Tammy Faye's makeup. And making up a few of my own.

Would I like to talk to Jim Bakker? No, thank you.

I knew all too well his story. By the mid 1980s, he had achieved the American dream as leader of the multi-million-dollar empires Heritage USA, PTL, and the Inspirational Network. He seemed to revel in the prestige, the power, and the adoration of millions. A premiere proponent of the Prosperity Gospel, Bakker preached an up-beat message of optimism, health, and wealth. Then, in 1987 his world caved in when a sexual encounter with

Jessica Hahn, a church secretary from New York, became international news. The loss of his reputation was only the beginning. Convicted in 1989 of mail and wire fraud for fund-raising efforts at PTL, the former confidant of presidents found himself sentenced to 45 years in a federal prison. Released after five years, Jim Bakker had just finished his memoirs, *I Was Wrong*, when his publicist called.

"Why won't you talk with him?" she asked. "He's doing very few interviews."

"I don't know," I replied, pausing. "I guess I'm pretty cynical. . . . How much money is he making from this book?"

"He can't receive any royalties because of taxes and litigation fees."

"Hmmmm . . . well, sure, I'll talk to him." I knew the conversation would be an interesting one. But I would never put it into print.

A few days later I find myself talking with a soft-spoken man, very different than the television persona I remember. One who has lost his wife, his dignity, and every penny he had. Barbara Walters has just left his house after a tear-filled interview, but I feel little emotion as I ask him why he wrote the book.

"I want my children, my grandchildren, and the people who supported and watched me for 25 years to understand what I learned in prison—that my previous philosophy of life was flawed," he says. "I once taught people not to pray 'Thy will be done,' when they want a new car, just claim it. I preached that God wanted everybody to be rich and prosperous, with no pain and no problems—a Pollyanna gospel. But the Prosperity Gospel doesn't make much sense when you're locked up in prison. As I studied the Bible there, I was appalled that I could have been so wrong, and I was deeply grateful that God had not struck me dead as a false prophet. I had taught people to fall in love with money. The deceitfulness of riches and the lust for other things had choked out the Word of God in my life and in the lives of my family members and coworkers. God does not promise riches nor prosperity, but He promises to never leave or forsake us, no matter what pain or trial we're going through."

"What changed your mind?" I ask.

"The words of Jesus. For two solid years in prison, I read and reread every word He said. I wrote them out countless times and studied them in the original Greek. As I began to study Jesus, I didn't find Him saying anything good about money. In Luke 6:24 He says, 'Woe to you who are rich. . . .' Matthew 6:19 says, 'Lay not up treasures on earth.' How could I be telling people to get rich?"

The reason was simple. Bakker preached selectively, skipping over verses or rationalizing them away. "Surely the love of money couldn't be the root of evil," he told himself. "Surely it was something more terrible, like murder or hatred." He says he preached "long-horned sermons"—a point here, a point there, and lots of bull in between. "I would take a verse from the Old Testament, a verse from the New, and put a lot of Jim Bakker in between. I took success books and put scriptures to them. I would get off on what's wrong with the government, on scaring people about this and that, but what people needed was the Word of God. In Matthew 7, Jesus said, 'Many will say unto me in that day, "Lord, Lord, have we not prophesied in thy name, cast out devils and in thy name done many wonderful works?" And He will say unto them, "Depart from me, I never knew you."' The Greek word for 'know' means an intimate relationship. Christ is not interested in our prophecies, in our huge bank accounts. I knew rich men who prophesied and lived like the devil. Jesus will say, 'I never knew them.' He has never had an intimate relationship with them. I should have taught people to fall in love with Jesus rather than the trappings."

At this point in our conversation, I am questioning my decision not to print the interview. "What is it about prison that radically transforms so many?" I ask.

"In prison you are forced to take a sabbath. I had five years of sabbaths. In a real way God brought me to prison to die, but not physically. He allowed me to be incarcerated so I could die to myself. In prison I came to the end of Jim Bakker."

"In what ways are you different today than before you went to prison?"

He answers softly, "Oh . . . I'm so different. I feel totally unworthy to stand in the pulpit. I don't have the ambitions I once had. I just live one day at a time. I want to be where God wants me. I don't have a reputation, so I don't have to prove anything to anybody. I can minister to anyone. Jesus could sit in the marketplace with a prostitute or at Matthew's house with criminals. He made Himself of no reputation. It's a marvelous place to be. I don't have a lot of bills, just my rent and utilities and groceries. I used to have to raise a million dollars every two days. That's pretty nice not to have over your head."

Tammy Faye's book *Telling It My Way* came off the presses almost the same day as Bakker's. I ask if he's read the book. He has. I ask what he thought. There is a pause.

A long pause. Then, finally, "I'm not sure I should say. My real feelings would be hurtful."

I respond as journalists are trained to: "My impressions were that her book could have been called *I Was Right*. Is that unfair?"

There is no pause this time. "I will not bad-mouth Tammy Faye. She's the mother of my children and I will always love her."

"Do you blame her for divorcing you?"

"I was facing 45 years in prison. She's someone who needs someone there every hour of every day to tell her she's loved. I carried her. I pampered her. I babied her for 30 years, so much of it is my fault, I guess. I take responsibility for the divorce. I went to prison. I made wrong decisions."

Quickly he changes the subject. Living on a farm in the house next to his daughter, he is finding that being with his grandchildren is the joy of his life. "The title of this book is not what you want for your memoirs; not what you'd like to pass on to your grandchildren. But my children are very gracious. They should be bitter and away from God, but both of them are serving Him full-time."

"Can God still use someone who has failed?" I ask.

He tells of a cold January morning when he was summoned from his cell. Sick with the flu and filthy from cleaning toilets, he reluctantly accompanied a guard to the warden's office. There a visitor was waiting. It was Billy Graham. "As I walked through the door, he turned toward me and opened his arms wide. Immediately I felt total acceptance and love. I wanted to run into his arms like a little boy would run into his daddy's arms. We talked for a while and when he left he told me he'd be praying for me.

I knew then that God loved me. That God could use me again. That's the grace of God."

"God has forgiven you. Do you ever wonder if Christians will?"

His voice grows even quieter. "Ministers told me that God didn't love me. So many Christians have harbored hatred towards me. I felt God hated me. But He said He will never, never leave me. The first thing I do at every service I go to is ask forgiveness of the people. The Bible says unless you forgive, you will not be forgiven. There are so many scriptures in the Bible about judging and not judging. If you judge, you'll be judged the same way. If you don't forgive, you'll not be forgiven. Unforgiveness kills the person who doesn't forgive."

"I need to ask your forgiveness, too," I say. "I . . . well, I never really liked Jim Bakker."

"I didn't either," he says with a smile. "But God did."

"Why would God allow you to lose everything and end up in prison?"

"Because He loves me. Those He loves He chastens. The Bible says the trial of your faith is more precious than gold. I had been telling people that if they had problems it was because they had sin in their lives. I was teaching them how not to 'become gold.' It was God's grace that took me to jail. In prison, a young bank robber asked me, 'Why does God hate me?' When I told him of God's love, he wasn't impressed. But months later he told me I was right. He said, 'I'd be dead if God hadn't intervened in my life.' If I would have kept on going, I would have ended up in a mental institution or at least totally burnt out. I would not go back to the way things were for anything. God used the circumstances of losing PTL to bring me to a place of genuine brokenness, repentance, and surrender. It hurt. And the losses my family and I have endured have been many and irreplaceable. But in the light of eternity, it will be worth it all."[15]

Although the final chapter has yet to be written, as I talk to Jim Bakker, I can't help but be reminded of another humbled sinner. One who failed his country and failed his God: King David. In both cases, the sinner found what amazes every one of us who falls and gets back up: God's amazing grace. It is truly the most wonderful gift that money can't buy.

CHAPTER TWENTY-SIX

What Money Can Buy

> *"He is richest who is content with the least."*
>
> —SOCRATES (470–399 B.C.)

RECENTLY ANN LANDERS GAVE READERS OF
her popular column an unusual assignment: write and tell
her what they had found while jogging. The assignment
was spurred on by a short letter Ann received from an
Indiana couple who for six years had made it their practice to look on the ground no matter where they went.
Their search paid off. "We now have 400 dollars in a container," they wrote. Incredibly, Craig Davidson of Phoenix
topped that story without a problem. He wrote claiming
he'd found 5,170 dollars while jogging. His wife verified
the claim. "He runs a lot more than the average jogger,"
she said.

When I was about five, I found a quarter on a sidewalk one morning (probably made more than my dad that
day!), and before rushing to the candy store, I ran home
to show it to my mother. "I'm gonna look for money

everywhere I go now," I told her, gasping for breath. My wise old mother sat me down and told me a story about a man who found a five-dollar bill in a gutter and spent the rest of his life looking for more. According to my mother, he never saw the trees. He never saw the flowers. He never saw the birds. In fact, he missed a hundred rainbows and a thousand sunsets. All he saw was gutters. "I hope you enjoy that candy, Philip," she said, "but remember . . . always look a little higher."

Here are the stories of some who have learned the joy of looking a little higher. Who are learning what a buck can—and cannot—buy.

———

"In my hurry to make it to work this morning, I ignored icy conditions, slid into a curb, and readjusted my truck's alignment. That was just the start of a horrible day. When I arrived home, my youngest greeted me at a decibel level only a parent could appreciate: 'Daddy, Daddy, Daddy.' Then I remembered my New Year's resolution: 'Look for the wealth of things God has blessed me with even in the midst of hard times.' I also recalled that when Matthew Henry was robbed, he wrote in his diary, 'Let me be thankful . . . first, because I was never robbed before . . . second, because although they took my wallet they did not take my life . . . third, because although they took my all, it was not much . . . and fourth, because it was I who was robbed, not I who did the robbing.'"

———

"Five years ago my husband and I had 11 credit cards and a debt of 100,000 dollars. Today we are debt-free. For us the steps to financial freedom were simple but not always easy. First we quit spending more than we were making. Then we had a melt-down-our-plastic party. Then we paid God first (about 15 percent), paid ourselves next (putting away 10 percent each month), and paid the bills with what was left. We've had to downsize our dreams a little, but the nightmares have gone away. We've even had enough to give to some needy friends. Our lives are far richer because of it."

"A few years ago our church sent a container of clothes to the Ukraine. We had a hundred dollars that we wanted to spend, so we found a store that would give us a good deal on a hundred dollars' worth of wool work socks. Giving money away has made my life richer."

"We're moving across town to the wrong side of the tracks this week. We're venturing into the Somali slums here in Nairobi. These past two years our lives have been richer because of these refugees. We have fed, clothed, and prayed with people who suffer daily more than I ever thought possible. In the discovery that life is harder than I'd ever imagined, I have also discovered that God is bigger and better than I'd ever imagined. We left a comfortable home in North America to offer the hope of eternity to suffering people. This has made our lives rich indeed."

"Right now I am a student and I am many thousands of dollars in debt. I do not have good prospects for a high-paying job. I do not own a home, a car, a dog, or a white picket fence. But if I were granted a wish I do not think I would ask for anything. Why? Because I have a loving wife and soon-to-be-born child. I am clothed, fed, and housed. I am doing what I most love to do. I have a network of caring and supportive relationships through friends and family. And I am an heir of God's grace. He satisfies my desires with good things. He has seen me thus far and He will see me home."

———

"A year ago we decided to quit eating out so much and use the money to support a needy child in Latin America through Compassion. We keep her picture in our dining room now and pray for her almost every night. Our daughters write her letters and consider her a part of our extended family. It's tough not to feel rich when you're giving money away."

———

"I noticed the other day that a widow in our town is working two jobs to make ends meet. As an author and speaker, I'm able to make some extra money, so we've started sending her what we can. She doesn't know about it, but our kids sure do. It's probably the only family secret we have. Every time I come back from speaking, the kids want to know . . . can we give more money to our widow friend?"

———

"A few days after our second child was born, my wife and I were carrying our newborn daughter, Jill, out of the hospital to take her home. An elderly man from our church was pacing the lobby. His wife was in the hospital dying of cancer and he spent most of his time with her.

"Walking up to us with a tired smile, he pressed a 20-dollar bill into my hand. 'My wife and I were never able to have children,' he said. 'But we hear you'll be needing lots of this. God bless you.' Four years have passed and he is a widower now. Whenever we see him sitting alone at church, our family sits beside him. I'm sure our kids are a little noisy sometimes, but he doesn't seem to mind. And one of them has even started calling him Grandpa. She's his favorite.

"She's our four-year-old, Jill."

Part V

RICH PEOPLE LEAVE THE RIGHT THINGS BEHIND

Spring is snowball season where I live. The warm west winds descend from the mountains to turn drifts into slush and adults into children. The other day on my way to work I was hit between the shoulder blades with a hard-packed ball of ice. Ouch. Turning around, I saw the culprit. A five-year-old with one hand clasped over her mouth. Perhaps she didn't think her aim was that good. I was in a hurry. Deadlines to meet. Phone calls to make. But for some reason, I bent down and fashioned a few weapons of my own. And for the next few minutes we engaged in a delightful battle. A battle which I lost. Quite badly.

Later the little girl's mother came to my office. She was a single mom. She'd had a tough day. The job she applied for didn't pan out. The car she needed she couldn't afford. But for a minute or two a snowball fight had helped lighten her load. "I want to thank you," she said with tears in her eyes. "My little girl has heard you preach, but I think she'll listen a little more carefully next time. And I think I will, too."

When we leave this earth, we won't take much. The U-Haul doesn't follow the hearse, they say. But I'm glad that we can leave a few things behind. We can leave footprints everywhere we go. Grace-full footprints. Footprints of encouragement. Of kindness. Of forgiveness. Of love. Footprints that others will want to follow.

Here are five stories of the things we leave behind.

CHAPTER TWENTY-SEVEN

Growing Up Fundagelical

"The law tells me how crooked I am. Grace comes along and straightens me out."

—D. L. MOODY (1837-1899)

I GREW UP IN A CONSERVATIVE COMMUNITY which some called Fundagelical. I realize the term may be a new one for you, so let me define it by saying that some in our congregation felt we shouldn't evangelize the Amish because they dressed a bit too flashy. Of course, I'm stretching things a little here, but my point is, regardless of which way the wind blew, we leaned a little to the right.

Sundays we worshiped and slept (sometimes simultaneously), Wednesdays we faithfully attended prayer meeting (unless our prayers were answered and my father forgot!), and Friday evenings we gathered around camp fires to sing choruses (unless Basic Youth Conflicts was in town).

We did not play cards (except Rook), attend movies (except *The Hiding Place*), or yell "Shoot!" (except during church basketball games). Most of our parents enjoyed George Beverly Shea's music until the percussion section got carried away, and we were taught to dance only when shot at with live ammunition.

I almost feel guilty mentioning it, but I had a great deal of fun growing up Fundagelical. Oh sure, there were negative side effects. For instance, there was the memory loss. And there was, uh . . . I can't remember the other thing. Seriously, certain side effects do linger. For one thing, I grew up with the strong impression that Christianity was largely outward. Though I often heard that works weren't the ticket to heaven, we found out early that it was our actions which gained approval (or disapproval) down here. The result was a tendency to fake my faith.

I also grew up believing God wanted me miserable. Don't ask me why. I guess I saw it in the faces of those who came to church looking like breakfast was a bowl of lemons with vinegar on the side. God's will for my life, I thought, included serving Him in the remotest part of India married to the girl who sat at the front of our class squealing on everyone. And so, reluctant to trust God with everything I had, I decided to pursue adventure elsewhere.

You didn't have to look far in those days.

For a mischievous Fundagelical child, it only took a spark to get a scandal going.

When I was ten, I invented recycling. I know it sounds improbable, but it's true. One August afternoon, a friend and I took a garbage bag to our town's main street and placed in it every cigarette butt we could find. Loudly we said, "Boy, are these ever disgusting. Can you believe people actually smoke these things?" And passersby nodded their approval. Such good children. Such conscientious children. There is hope for the next generation after all.

We smiled and thanked them for their comments. Then we carried the garbage bag to our fort in the woods. And we recycled those cigarettes. Every last one of them. Right down to the filters. In fact, we recycled pretty much anything we could get our lips around that summer. Tea leaves. Pencil shavings. Cinnamon. Cardboard. You name it, we sat in the weeds and inhaled it.

One fine Wednesday our dreams came true. Discarded in a deserted ditch was the desire of our hearts: a pack of Player's Filter Tip, unopened and beckoning. Stripping the plastic off, we divided the pack evenly. Ten apiece. And we sat in the tall weeds inhaling every last one of them. Right down to the filters.

After staggering back to the nonsmoking zone, my friend was caught yellow-handed by his mother. But I was older. I was wiser. I knew that as ye smoke, so shall ye reek. Plus my brother Tim had told me the punishment for smoking in our community: "They cut your lips off." So I slipped silently up to our medicine cabinet and found a can of spray deodorant. I finished it. Then I pulled out a full tube of toothpaste. I finished that, too. Finally I was able to approach my parents.

"My, do you smell nice, Son."

"Thank you," I said. "Thank you very much."

And that night I crawled into bed, a satisfied smile stuck to my face. *Boy, are you brilliant,* I thought. *No one will ever know.*

My mother entered the room then and sat on my bed, sniffing. "How did it taste?" she asked.

"Uh . . . supper? Very good, Mom. Thank you. Thank you very much."

"When I was a little girl," she continued, without skipping a beat, "Grandpa let me smoke his pipe. I didn't much like it. How about you?"

She could have cut my lips off. Or spanked me. Or quoted Scripture. She could have reminded me that no amount of toothpaste or deodorant will cover our sins. That they really will find us out. She could have reminded me that the story doesn't end there. That because of what Jesus did on the cross, we don't have to hide. We can approach God, forever forgiven. Instead she leaned over and kissed me gently on the forehead.

"I'll never smoke again," I said. Then, "Mom, how did you know?"

"Well, Son," she said, tucking the covers in around my shoulders, "sometimes ten-year-old boys forget that their mothers have friends, too."

And I heard my father's voice, coming from the bathroom. "Hey, has anyone seen the deodorant?"

Looking back on my childhood, I'm thankful for rules. I'm thankful I learned early about the seriousness of sin. But I'm glad I was shown more. I'm glad I was shown grace.

Today I have three children of my own (who said God doesn't have a sense of humor?) and I'm spending more time on my knees than ever before. Last July I turned 35, a fact my ten-year-old son won't let me forget. "You're half dead, you know," he told me as I tucked the covers in around his shoulders. After grounding him until his sixteenth birthday, I realized that his response came from a Bible verse that estimates our allotted time on earth to be threescore and ten years. *The boy knows all the right verses,* I thought. Then I remembered fellow classmates who scored 100 percent on every Bible memory test, only to abandon the faith. And I knelt by his bed and prayed for my kids.

I prayed that they will discover early that rules are necessary, that Christians are human, and that God's will is the very best thing. I prayed that they will love the Lord Jesus with everything they've got.

But mostly I prayed that they will breathe deeply of grace. And discover, as I have, that we travel a little lighter when God's grace carries us along.

CHAPTER TWENTY-EIGHT

One Flew Over the Teacher's Desk

"A teacher affects eternity; he can never tell where his influence stops."

—HENRY BROOKS ADAMS (1838–1918)

WELL, IT'S BEEN QUITE A WEEK. ON WEDNESday the children brought home their report cards. On Thursday we went to see their teachers and beg for forgiveness. Sometimes at night, as we sit around the dinner table, I ask the kids, "So, what did you learn today?" Almost without exception, they respond: "Nothing."

This week we had tangible proof that they were telling the truth.

They say that the world will never be a better place until children are an improvement on their parents, and I must admit that though my kids' marks leave a little to be desired, they are a dramatic improvement on mine.

I was a problem child during my school days. In fact, if you were to check the records at Prairie Elementary

School, you would discover that I still hold the record for Most Whippings in a Week. If you doubt me, you can talk to my teachers. I believe a few of them lived to tell about it. Of course, I am not proud of this. But let me take the next few minutes to tell you all about those years. And of a teacher who literally changed my life.

————

On my very first day of school, Leslie Kolibaba squealed on me for having my eyes open during prayer (yes, they prayed back then), and teachers viewed me with suspicion from that day onward. By grade three, teachers were already wondering if there was any hope for me. I was known as a kid who couldn't keep quiet, who couldn't keep still, and who couldn't keep from asking far too many questions. I'm sure when they looked around the classroom, they experienced the same anxiety every teacher experiences: Are these kids learning anything at all?

The answer is obvious: No. As proof, here are a few things students have written on tests and essays over the years:

- Benjamin Franklin invented electricity by rubbing cats backward and declared "a horse divided against itself cannot stand." Franklin died in 1790 and is still dead.
- Handel, the famous composer, was half German, half Italian, and half English.
- Bach died from 1750 to the present.
- Beethoven was so deaf he wrote loud music. He expired in 1827 and later died for this.
- Queen Victoria was the longest queen. She sat on a thorn for 63 years. Her death was the final event which ended her reign.

- Socrates died from an overdose of wedlock.
- William Shakespeare was famous for writing and per-
  forming tragedies, comedies, and hysterectomies.
* Christopher Columbus circumcised the earth with a
  100-foot clipper.
- Our new teacher taught us all about fossils. Before she
  came to class I didn't know what a fossil looked like.

By the time I reached high school, I wished for all the
world that I could quit. After all, my marks had been slipping ever since kindergarten and few held any hope that I
would amount to anything.

To complicate matters, there were some strange
teachers roaming the classrooms. One prided himself on
calling everyone by birthday. I was July 26. A friend of
mine was May 3. "Hi, May 3," he'd say, walking past us in
the hall. Or, "July 26, would you stand and read paragraph
three from page 220?"

Several years after high school my friend and his new
bride were walking around a mall 1000 miles from home,
and they happened to meet this former teacher. They
stopped to talk with him. But all he said was "Hi, May 3,"
then he walked away. Needless to say, this dear man's ele-
vator wasn't stopping at all the right floors, and I can't remember a thing I learned from him. Except I never forget
my friend's birthday.

Thankfully we had other teachers too.

In tenth grade, I was standing at the drinking fountain swapping jokes with friends, when my English
teacher, Mr. Bienert, came along. Taking me aside, he
spoke some simple words that have changed my life.
Later I discovered that he'd been in the faculty lounge

talking to some of the other teachers, all of whom were wondering if there was any hope for me.

"Listen, Callaway," said Mr. Bienert, "your math marks aren't adding up. Your gift at science has yet to be discovered. Biology? Chemistry? Physics? Well, the experiment is not working."

I'd been told this before.

This was not news to me.

But what he said next was the best news I'd heard in a long time: "I want you in my Communication Arts class. I think God has given you a gift in the area of communication."

The very next day I had no trouble getting out of bed. I even put on matching clothes. And after joining his class, I worked eagerly on my very first assignment: writing a poem for a poetry contest. I can't remember a word I wrote, but I'll never forget Mr. Bienert standing at the front of the classroom, pulling five bucks from his wallet, and calling me forward.

"Congratulations, Callaway. You've got first prize," he said, stuffing the bill into my eager hand. "I want you to read this in chapel tomorrow. It's good stuff."

The next day my knees knocked and my hands shook, as I walked to the podium. But I read that poem loudly before the entire school.

All because someone believed in me.

You know, I've been influenced by a whole lot of people over the years. Some have scolded me. Some have hollered at me. Some have spanked me. And most have forgotten my birthday. But I want you to remember this: Those who influenced me the most are not those who pointed out all my faults, but those who knew that God was bigger than my shortcomings. Those who influenced me the most didn't just point a finger, they held out a helping hand.

None of us knows what God will do when we encourage someone, do we? I almost flunked French class in high school. Now they're translating my writings into languages like Polish, Spanish, Chinese, and English (one of which I speak fluently). I was born with a face for radio, but a new video series of mine is being distributed in 63,000 churches around the world.

This is no tribute to me.

It is a tribute to the goodness and greatness of God. And it's a tribute to those, like Mr. Bienert, who believed in God enough to believe in me.

We may forget some birthdays. But let's not forget to encourage someone. Today.

CHAPTER TWENTY-NINE

Walk with Me

> *"Jesus wants us to see that the neighbor next door
> or the people sitting next to us on a plane or in
> a classroom are not interruptions to our schedule.
> They are there by divine appointment. Jesus wants
> us to see their needs, their loneliness, their longings,
> and He wants to give us the courage to reach out
> to them."*
>
> —REBECCA MANLEY PIPPERT

SOMEONE HAS SAID THAT CHRISTIANS AND non-Christians have something in common. We're both uptight about evangelism. That's me. Uptight. I have to admit that most of the people in my life are Christians. Too often I'm too busy or too uptight to interact with people who do not share my view of the world. But lately I'm beginning to understand that I don't have to be Billy Graham to have an impact. I don't have to be Josh McDowell to have an answer. In fact, it's okay to be myself.

On a long flight to Dallas recently, I found myself seated beside a psychologist. Within five minutes of take-off he had correctly diagnosed me as a Christian. "I've had lots of bad experiences with Christians," he confided.

"Really?" I said, rather excitedly. "Me too."

He laughed at my response, and soon began talking about his family, his life, and his job. "I counsel people with a rare disease. I'm sure you haven't heard of it," he said. "It's called Huntington's." *Wow*, I thought. *This is probably the biggest surprise I ever want to experience on an airplane.*

"Huntington's? Oh, boy," I said, "That's . . . well, pretty close to home." For the next four hours we discussed the role Huntington's had played on my journey into trust. We spoke of our favorite sports teams and the human condition. We talked of airline omelets and the Bible. "I grew up in the church and I've been turned off by religion," he said, pouring himself another drink. "Me too," I answered. "I tried it for a while, but it's a lousy substitute for a relationship with Jesus." He turned my way. "This may sound crazy to a psychologist," I told him, "but I'm not sure where I'd be today if I didn't live in constant communication with Someone I can't even see."

He smiled and shook his head slowly. "No," he said. "In my experience, it's not crazy at all."

When we parted ways, he kept shaking his head. "You've given me a few things to think about," he told me. I assured him that he had done the same for me.

Sometimes I wish I had more answers.

Sometimes I wish I had more charisma.

But I'm beginning to understand that what people need more than either of these is reality. The reality of a relationship that affects the way we respond to everything around us.

Joni Eareckson Tada, who has spent most of her life in a wheelchair following a diving accident, once said, "Nothing will convince and convict those around us like the peaceful and positive way we respond to our hurts and distress. The unbelieving world—your neighbors, the guy at the gas station, the postman, the lady at the cleaners, your boss at work—is observing the way we undergo our trials." And, I might add, the way we respond to the trials of others.

A few years ago, a simple story had a profound impact on me. Two neighbors were as different as day and night in the way they looked at the world. One was a lifelong Democrat, the other a Republican. One was a solid Christian, the other wouldn't darken a church door if his life depended on it. But for some reason they got along. They knew that discussing business or politics or religion was a surefire formula for disaster, so they stuck with talking about their marriages, their kids, and the yard work. When the non-Christian's wife was diagnosed with a virulent form of cancer and died in three short months, it was his Christian neighbor who stepped in.

Recalling the night of his wife's death, the husband wrote, "I was in total despair. I went through the funeral preparations and the service like I was in a trance. And that night after the service, I just wanted to be alone. I left and went to the path along the river in our town and walked all night. But I did not walk alone. My neighbor, afraid for me, I suppose, stayed with me all night. He did not speak; he did not try and get me to go home; he did not even walk beside me. He just followed me. When the sun finally came up over the river the next morning, he came up to me and said, 'Let's get some breakfast.'

"I go to church now, my neighbor's church. I do not really like the pastor's politics sometimes. But a religion that can produce the kind of caring and love my neighbor showed me is something I want to be involved in. I want to be like that. I want to love and be loved like that the rest of my life."[16]

We may not have all the answers, but each of us is capable of this much. In a world characterized by loneliness and despair, we can reach out in love to those around us. Or, as St. Francis once said, we can "preach the gospel all the time; if necessary, use words."

Looking back, I have to admit that most of my attempts to tell others of Jesus have seemed like a failure. What I fail to realize is that God is more than capable of making up for my inadequacies. This was never more clear to me than the cold winter night in Hamilton, Ontario, when I met Michael.

CHAPTER THIRTY

Two Things Last Forever

"Moses wasn't qualified to lead God's people out of Egypt. He spoke with a stutter. He was reluctant and unwilling and he couldn't control his temper. . . . In a very real sense not one of us is qualified, but it seems that God continually chooses the most unqualified to do His work. . . . If we are qualified, we tend to think that we have done the job ourselves. If we are forced to accept our evident lack of qualification, then there's no danger that we will confuse God's work with our own."

—MADELEINE L'ENGLE

AT THE AGE OF 26, MICHAEL SLADE IS A NEO-Nazi skinhead who enjoys reading the works of Aldous Huxley and Adolf Hitler. If you saw the two of us together, you might take a second look. Then a third.

In his place of employment, Michael is paid to be irritable. In fact, the more irritable he gets, the better his results. Michael, you see, is a bill collector. Over the phone he intimidates people, and in the evenings he relies on alcohol and drugs to take the edge off. Most weekends he moves in with a 38-year-old divorcée and her two small children.

A neighbor invited Michael to a Saturday-night meeting where I was speaking and for some reason he came along. Afterwards Michael wandered over to where I was standing. With one hand he fingered a cigarette pack, with the other he thumbed through one of my books. When he bought it, I wrote in the front: "To Michael, Philippians 1:9,10." You may remember the verses: "And this is my prayer: that your love may abound more and more in knowledge and depth of insight, so that you may be able to discern what is best and may be pure and blameless until the day of Christ."

"Do you have a Bible?" I asked.

"Ya. But I haven't read it yet."

"When you get home tonight will you read these verses?"

He said he would. Then he was gone.

The next day on the flight home I prayed for Michael. I knew I would never see him again, but for some reason I couldn't get him off my mind. Perhaps it was the frustration I felt from knowing I hadn't said the right thing, or given him the right verses. I was too busy selling books.

That night I fell asleep praying for Michael.

The following Wednesday the phone rang. You guessed it. Bill collectors can track you down anywhere, and I was glad he had. "I read your book through without stopping," he began. "I laughed, I cried, and I . . . I just had to talk to you." On Saturday after the meeting, Michael went home and somehow found Philippians. He started to read it and he couldn't stop. "I told my girlfriend we've been doing some stuff we shouldn't be doin'," he said. On Sunday night Michael couldn't sleep. He paced the floor. "Then," he told me, "I heard my name called out loud. Twice. I woke up my roommate but it wasn't him." All that week Michael had trouble thinking about anything else.

As we talked, Michael gave me a firsthand account of one who spent his life desperately seeking pleasure only to come up empty. "I've made a mess of my life," he said. "If I, like, come to God, will He make me comfortable?"

I paused for a moment. "No," I said, "God won't make you comfortable." I tried to recite C. S. Lewis' words: "I didn't go to religion to make me happy. I always knew a bottle of port would do that. If you want a religion to make you feel really comfortable, I certainly don't recommend Christianity."

Lewis went on to say, "The Christian religion does not begin in comfort; it begins in dismay. . . . Comfort is the one thing you cannot get by looking for it. If you look for truth, you may find comfort in the end: If you look for comfort you will not get either comfort or truth—only wishful thinking . . . and, in the end, despair."[17]

Michael was silent for a minute. I told him how difficult the last few years of my life had been. That God had not taken our problems away. He had sent His Holy Spirit, the Comforter, to help us carry them. I told him about Jesus' death on the cross, the end of a life which could not be described as comfortable. About the Bible's account of His resurrection and the difference it had made in my life.

Again, Michael was silent.

Before we hung up I tried to show him how to find the Gospel of John (you should try this sometime over the phone). "Read right through it," I said, "and ask yourself this question, 'Who is Jesus?' "

That night I went to sleep praying for Michael. This time I was sure I wouldn't hear back. After all, my words had faltered. I hadn't always said what I meant. And what I had said was anything but popular. People don't get all excited about things like crucifixion. About lack of comfort. About carrying crosses. And repenting of sin. But once again I underestimated the power of God's Word. For you see, Sunday night Michael called again. This time we talked about his job, about his girlfriend, about sex, drugs, and rock 'n' roll. But mostly we talked about Jesus. Then we prayed together and Michael asked Christ to be the biggest part of his life.

We were 2000 miles apart, but closer than we'd ever been before.

When I wrote my first book I told God that the midnights alone in front of the computer would be well worth it if just one person was in heaven as a result. He heard my prayer that Sunday night. He delights in doing that. Through me. Through you. Through all who realize that this world and everything in it will one day pass away, but two things will last forever: God's Word and people.

The richest life you'll ever live will be invested in these.

CHAPTER THIRTY-ONE

The Stuff We Leave Behind

"The great use of life is to spend it for something that outlasts it."

—WILLIAM JAMES (1842–1910)

WELL, I FINALLY DID IT. AFTER YEARS OF checking out prices, I talked myself into buying one. After years of admiring those tiny leaves and gnarled branches, I mustered up the courage to bring one home. It sits in my living-room window now. Soaking up the sun's rays. Reaching out for moisture. And growing . . . ever so slowly.

I didn't know they existed until I watched a movie called *The Karate Kid.* The wise old master pruned and wired and clipped away, then one day presented a lonely and mistreated boy with an ancient tree ten inches tall. The tree spoke to the boy of endurance, of perseverance, of growth—things he would need to bring the movie to a happy end. Since then, I've wanted a bonsai tree for myself. But they looked too much like work (all that wiring

173

and clipping). They looked too much like money (some were as much as 1000 dollars). A few months ago, however, I found a small one for only 16 dollars, and it made no sense to leave it in the store.

Please understand that I wasn't born with a green thumb. In fact, if you have a plant you don't like, give it to me. I don't know what it is. I water and weed with the best of them, but plants see me coming and they change color. I walk by and they wilt. Things will be different with this tree, though. Some nights, after the kids are tucked in, you'll find me with the perfect pruning instrument (my wife's fingernail clippers), lovingly snipping, trimming, and wiring until it's all I can see when I close my eyes.

If the lady who sold me this tree is right, a well-cared-for bonsai should last a few hundred years. "Even longer than me," I told her. So I'll keep snipping, trimming, and wiring, and perhaps this tree will be around long after I've hung up the fingernail clippers. Of course, I'd like to leave behind a little more than a gnarled old tree, but after a story I heard this morning, I'm wondering what could be more important.

Just last summer, an acquaintance of mine took his 12-year-old son on a weekend fishing trip. The purpose was to teach the boy the facts of life. To let him know the wonderful joys of married love. "Sex is a gift from God to be celebrated and saved for the one you marry," he told his son, as they stood waist-deep in a crystal-clear stream, casting flies after rainbow trout.

The boy had no reason to doubt him. Not until a month later, when his dad walked out the front door with the same suitcase he'd taken along on that fishing trip. He left behind a devastated family. He left behind the awful truth: For over a year he'd been having an affair with a married woman. His boy may never be the same.

Since I heard the news, I've been thinking about the stuff we leave behind. You see, whether we like it or not, the impact we make is rarely determined by the words we say, but by the life we live. Those who impact us most are not those who preach to us, but those who live their lives quietly, gracefully, and faithfully, like the stars in the heavens.

Later this week, I'm going back to that store. Later this week, I'll buy three more bonsai trees. One for each of my kids.

Perhaps years from now in some far-off place, they'll be able to look at a bonsai basking in their living-room window, and think of their dad.

My son Stephen is 11 now. Going on 12. Soon to be 18. On his eighteenth birthday I hope to present him with a bonsai tree. Long after his birthday, he'll still have that tree. Long after my words have stopped ringing in his ears, he'll have a small reminder of the stuff that mattered to me.

I pray that the tree will speak to him of character.

Of perseverance.

Of faithfulness.

I hope it will remind him that although his dad had his share of twists and bends, he grew strong and faithful. Under the loving hand of the Master.

Part VI

RICH PEOPLE HAVE THE LAST LAUGH

Five years ago, within the space of two months, a friend of mine lost both of his sons, David and Andrew, to muscular dystrophy. Not long before David died, a schoolmate agreed to push him through a mall one Saturday. "If you could have just one wish, what would it be?" the friend asked, as they sat together watching frenzied shoppers. Trapped in a wheelchair, unable to move his arms and legs, David replied, "Nothing. I've got Jesus. My mom and dad love me. And I've got guys like you to help me over the speed bumps."

Then, smiling that awkward smile his friends and family had come to love, he added quietly, "Besides, I know where I'm going. And there ain't no wheelchairs there."

You know, I've met millionaires and billionaires. I've talked to CEOs and VIPs. But I've never met anyone richer than David.

Trapped in a wheelchair.

With no wishes.

But lots of hope.

CHAPTER THIRTY-TWO

Good News for Weary Travelers

"You gave me everything to live with, and nothing to live for."

—A TEENAGER'S SUICIDE NOTE TO HIS PARENTS

ON A TRAIN TRIP YEARS AGO MARK TWAIN found himself seated next to someone with the gift of gloom. The fellow traveler, reflecting on all that was wrong with the world, said to Twain, "Do you realize that every time I take a breath, 10,000 people on this planet die?"

Mark Twain thought for a minute, then replied, "Hmmmm . . . ever try cloves?"

Have you ever sat beside such a person? I did the other day. We were over Colorado, cruising at 31,000 feet, and he kept bringing me down to earth. Life as a government employee was giving him more than his share of ulcers, and to complicate matters, he suffered from a serious numbing of the funny bone. Flipping through a magazine, he showed me some appalling statistics. Frowning through a diet Coke, he told me of the moral chaos. "Things are bad all over," he said as a young child with a "No Fear" ball cap tried unsuccessfully to play peekaboo with him. "I give the world five years before the next Big Bang. Maybe six. You just watch."

Although I'm normally a mild-mannered sort (even more so when I've swallowed a motion-sickness pill), I thought I'd better say something. "Yes, the times are bad," I told him, "but they're the only times we have. If the Big Bang comes, I hope it finds me doing something productive. Dating my wife. Playing catch with my kids. Maybe planting a tree."

He didn't say anything, so I offered him a stick of gum (didn't have any cloves) and sat thinking about his comments. I couldn't argue with him. I read the news. I watch the television.

In fact, the previous night in my hotel room the film *City Slickers* was showing. In the film, comedian Billy Crystal plays the part of a bored salesman who is invited to his son's school to tell the children about his work. When Crystal stands up in the classroom, he launches into a deadpan monologue which bewilders the kids but has the rest of us smiling.

> Value this time in your life, kids, because this is the time in your life when you still have your choices. It goes by so fast.
>
> When you're a teenager, you think you can do anything and you do. Your twenties are a blur. Thirties you raise your family, you make a little money, and you think to yourself, "What happened to my twenties?"

Forties you grow a little pot belly, you grow another chin. The music starts to get too loud, one of your old girlfriends from high school becomes a grandmother. Fifties, you have a minor surgery—you'll call it a procedure, but it's a surgery.

Sixties, you'll have a major surgery, the music is still loud, but it doesn't matter because you can't hear it anyway.

Seventies, you and the wife retire to Fort Lauderdale. You start eating dinner at 2:00 in the afternoon, you have lunch around 10:00, breakfast the night before, spend most of your time wandering around malls looking for the ultimate soft yogurt and muttering, "How come the kids don't call? How come the kids don't call?"

The eighties, you'll have a major stroke, and you end up babbling with some Jamaican nurse who your wife can't stand, but who you call "Mama."

Any questions?

What a vivid picture of an empty life. A life without meaning. A life that seems to shout, "Hey, why go on? Where's the hope?"

Recently, the world's most infamous boxer seemed to shout this question. Sitting alone on a white leather couch, he told a television interviewer of the hopelessness of his life. With marble staircases rising behind him and diamond-studded rings adorning his hands, he talked of his boredom. Behind him ornate columns rose from a tranquil pool, and everywhere there were signs that since earning 75 million dollars in 1996, he had denied himself no pleasure. Built on 17 acres, his 61-room estate is the largest house in Connecticut. It boasts 38 baths, 7 kitchens, a disco, a gym, and a master bedroom with 5 television sets. It is one of four mansions the disgraced boxing legend owns around the world.

Yet for Mike Tyson life is meaningless.

When he confessed this to the interviewer, his words were met with a bewildered stare. "You have all this and you feel that way . . . ?" asked the reporter, raising an eyebrow. "Ya," said Tyson. "I stayed here probably four times . . . I guess I am extremely bored."

In another honest interview, pop star Boy George admitted, "Growing up, you dream of being liked and being successful. You imagine that fame can fill your needs. You just think, let me scale that pinnacle. But nothing outside yourself can make you feel whole. Not fame, not sex, not drugs, not money. None of those things work. Nothing can fill you up. And believe me—'cause I've tried them all. In some ways, I am the modern Elvis."

Have you ever felt like Mike Tyson or Boy George? Have the winds of hopelessness blown your way? If so, listen to the words of Leo Tolstoy, the Russian author of *War and Peace*. Like Mike Tyson, he achieved worldwide acclaim. Like Boy George, he searched everywhere for meaning, only to come up empty. But then he made a simple discovery that changed everything: "I began to draw near to the believers among the poor, simple, and ignorant, the pilgrims, monks, and peasants. The more I contemplated the lives of these simple folk, the more deeply was I convinced of the reality of their faith . . . for it alone gave life a meaning and made it worth living. . . . I felt that I had only truly lived when I believed in God. God is life. Live to seek God, and life will not be without Him. The light that then shone never left me. . . . I came to know that God is all we need."

I must confess that there are days when I feel like my fellow traveler. After all, you don't have to be a government employee to see that the outlook is not so good. But then I'm reminded that in the darkest of times, hope can shine the brightest.

Is hope a pie-in-the-sky illusion? Does it make us complacent, content to leave the world as it is?

I used to think so.

Until I sat down beside another traveler on the darkest voyage of all.

A voyage that would change him—and me—forever.

CHAPTER THIRTY-THREE

Divine Mathematics

"Life is an onion. You peel it off one layer at a time, and sometimes you weep."

—CARL SANDBURG (1878–1967)

I STOOD LOOKING OUT OUR FRONT WINDOW AT the morning rain and shaking my head. How could it be? My friend and mentor's only child. His teenage daughter. Gone. Days before she had wrestled on the carpet with our kids. Days before she had been so full of life. But last night all that changed. Last night after church she joined a carload of friends driving down the highway singing, "Soon and very soon we are goin' to see the King. . . ." Suddenly headlights burst in their faces and two of them were ushered into the presence of the King.

My own daughter, Rachael, was pulling at my sleeve now. "Daddy," she asked, "why are you crying?"

"It's Janella, Honey. She's with Jesus." The words seemed distant. Detached. Too implausible to be real.

"But if she's in heaven, why are you sad?"

"Ah, Rachael—"

The phone rang. It was Paul, the newly bereaved father. "The grief comes and goes in waves," he told me. "Right now I don't see how I can go on. What is there to live for?"

What could I say? My friend. Always joyful. So quick to laugh. So ready with a bear hug. Now . . . crying like a baby.

A year ago in this same kitchen he had talked to me about living every moment as if it were our last. Picking up a banana, he had given it a swift karate chop, then cleaned up the mess while my wife stood by, grinning and shaking her head. That same day he ate a live cricket just to watch us squirm. "We did this in Haiti all the time," he said, speaking of his days as a missionary kid. "North American crickets aren't bad, either. A little on the skinny side though." But today there was no laughter. Today we wept together and said very little.

Three months passed.

Three months in a wilderness of pain and loneliness and deep depression. Then one day, Paul and his wife, Judy, heard a knock at the door. A representative from World Exchange Program who had heard of their loss had a question: Would they be interested in hosting a 17-year-old student from Luxembourg? "He's been waiting for two years," she pleaded. "Soon he'll be too old for the program. He's paid his money and I want him in a Christian host family." Her enthusiasm seemed foreign to the emptiness in their hearts. "It's only a ten-month commitment."

Sitting at the kitchen table, they listened with growing sympathy for this 17-year-old. His name was Yves. His mother had died when he was only seven. His father when he was 14. Reviewing Yves's application, they noticed that he was allergic to dogs and cats. And they saw his comment on religion: "No interest. An atheist."

Against the advice of others to make no major decisions for a year, they found themselves at the airport one August evening, waiting with mixed emotions, to welcome a stranger into their home.

The next morning Yves accompanied his hosts to a predominantly black church, vibrant with enthusiasm. *What did I get myself into?* he wondered. *They're into some strange cult.*

Life at school was just as bewildering. Strange surroundings. Strange people. Strange language. Finally, Yves enrolled in a public-speaking class. His first assignment: Give a speech in front of his tough high-school peers. In the process of correcting his grammar, Paul read of Yves's admiration for the way they were handling the loss of their daughter, and his admission, "I'm beginning to think about God."

Neither Paul nor Judy knew much about raising boys, nor did they know that a year earlier, in the grip of depression, Yves had scribbled out a note: "God, if You're real, get me out of Luxembourg and find me a family."

One night while eating dessert together, Paul and Judy talked about Janella. "I picture her in heaven now, cheering us on," said Paul. As they talked, the conversation moved to Yves, and they were shocked to discover that both wanted to adopt him. And something deep inside them said it was the right thing to do.

And so, while the three did dishes together one evening, Paul popped the question. "Yves, how would you like to be adopted?" Smothering them in a soapy hug, Yves began to cry.

Judy took to mothering with enthusiasm, but Paul found himself struggling to give his new son a place in his heart. Painful reminders of Janella played havoc with his emotions and he wanted to withdraw from Yves.

One dark winter morning at 1:30, they were roused from a pleasant sleep as their new son danced into the room. "Wake up! Wake up!" he shouted. "It's true. He came in!"

Though Paul and Judy hadn't pushed their faith on him, Yves had heard a clear message: No matter how dark the night, a relationship with Jesus Christ gives us hope for the future. He had knelt that very night and been adopted. Once again.

As winter turned to spring, Yves's younger brother, Mike, came for a visit. On the third day of Mike's visit, Paul asked the question the new family had discussed before Mike's arrival: "How would you like to join our family and be our second son?" His face registered amazement and confusion. In Luxembourg an unrelated family never adopts a teenager, let alone two. He would think it over.

Later in the summer, Mike returned for a second visit. On the night before his return to Luxembourg, he embraced Judy and with tears streaming down his face said, "Congratulations, Mom." Then giving Paul a polite and reserved hug, he said, "Congratulations, Dad." The following January, he arrived to begin a new life.

February sunshine streamed through the kitchen window one Saturday morning, and Judy's homemade pancakes smothered in maple syrup beckoned from the table. Paul had just opened his mouth to ask the blessing, when Mike said, "Dad, can I pray?" Curiosity flashed across three faces. "Dear Lord," he began in a thick German accent, "tank you for da beautiful night, especially for me. . . ." *What could be next?* they wondered. "I asked You into my heart and YOU CAME IN!" Pancakes were forgotten and tears flowed again, as they all jumped up to hug him.

Before long, Mike's adoption was official.

In less than a year, the Steinhauer family had doubled.

One Sunday morning, as the new family sat together listening to the sermon, Paul's pastor moved away from his pulpit, looked at them with a smile, and began talking of God's divine mathematics. "Only God could take one and add two!" he said.

How true, agrees Paul. "Only God could take a grief so wrenching you want to end it all and transform it into a joy that makes you want to start all over again. As for God, His way is perfect."

Some wonder if the hope of heaven causes one to live a life detached from the real world down here. Paul and Judy give testimony to the opposite. Those who do the most for this world are those who think most of the next.

Yves would agree. As he said one day in the kitchen: "When I get to heaven, two things I will do. First, see Jesus face-to-face. Then, find Janella and thank her for making room for me in this family."

CHAPTER THIRTY-FOUR

Aging Grace

"When I was 40, my doctor advised me that a man in his forties shouldn't play tennis. I heeded his advice carefully and could hardly wait until I reached 50 to start again."

—HUGO BLACK, SUPREME COURT JUSTICE

LET ME ASK YOU A QUESTION. IT'S BEEN ON MY mind since a friend asked it during our biweekly gathering of the Circle of Six. If you haven't heard of us yet, allow me to explain that we are six handsome middle-aged men who get together every other Tuesday to sample chocolate cheesecakes and consider deep questions such as, "I wonder if we should go on a diet?"

Of course we discuss other things, too. Lately, for instance, we've been talking about the aging process.

The discussion started with an interesting question. A question I'd like you to consider.

Do you look forward to growing old?

Of course, all of us in the Circle of Six had a different answer. Personally, I did my best to avoid the question as long as I could by stuffing my mouth full of cheesecake. *Age is relative,* I thought. Fifty is old when you're 15, but not when you're 90. Furthermore, aging is the one thing we can't do anything about. If we're alive, we're aging (some of us more swiftly than others). But when I ran out of cheesecake, I had to answer the question. I had to admit that I don't look forward to growing old.

I'm not alone on this one. Just last week I watched a "20/20" story on a European woman who is spending her 100,000-dollar inheritance trying to look like a human version of Barbie. So far she has undergone over 100 plastic surgeries. But just like you and me, she is aging.

When faced with the prospect of growing older, others have responded in different ways. "Age is mind over matter," joked the boxer Muhammad Ali. "As long as you don't mind, it doesn't matter." Baseball Hall of Famer Joe DiMaggio admitted that when you get older "you start chasing a ball and your brain immediately commands your body to 'Run forward! Bend! Scoop up the ball! Peg it to the infield!' Then your body says, 'Who, me?'" When asked what it's like to grow old, Babe Ruth put it bluntly, "It's hell to get older."

How about you? Would you agree with the Babe?

Before you answer, consider for a minute some who paint an entirely different picture of the aging process. Although not on the level of Noah, who became the father of three after turning 500 and completed the ark 100 years later, recent history is replete with the names of those who refuse to act their age. Those who, like the aging mosquito, aren't content to wait for an opening. They get in there and make one. Here are just a few:

- At 75, Charles Schultz, the creator of the "Peanuts" comic strip, still played ice hockey.
- Leo Tolstoy learned to ride a bicycle at 67 and wrote "I Cannot Be Silent" at 82.
- When he was 90, Eamon de Valera served as president of Ireland.
- Alexander Graham Bell was 84 when he produced the telephone.
- Claude Monet began painting his famous Water Lily series at age 76. And finished the work at age 85.
- In their 90s, pianist Arthur Rubenstein and cellist Pablo Casals both performed professionally.
- Roget was updating his famous thesaurus when he died at age 90.
- At 94, Leopold Stokowski signed a six-year recording contract.
- At 70, Amos Alonzo Stagg retired as football coach at the University of Chicago and became coach of a small California college. He produced a winning team, was named Coach of the Year, and was still coaching advisor at age 98.
- At 91, George Bernard Shaw was still writing plays.
- At 100, Grandma Moses was still painting pictures.
- And Tesichi Igarishi celebrated his hundredth birthday by climbing to the 12,395-foot-high summit of Mount Fuji.

Recently I asked Gordon MacDonald, the author of numerous bestsellers including *Ordering Your Private World,* what separates those who age gracefully from those who don't. Gordon, who just turned 59 (old to me!), told me that the elderly people he admires most share seven characteristics that have made their lives rich.

1. They are thankful people. Their conversation and their correspondence are marked with appreciation.
2. They show enthusiastic interest in the accomplishments of the younger generation. Change is not their enemy but their friend.
3. They keep their minds sharp and agile. Theirs is not the world of yesterday, but today.
4. They are big-picture people. They look at life from the largest point of view, resisting panic when sudden events grab the headlines.
5. They never retire. They may slow down and walk away from a job, but they still live life with a mission.
6. They are servants. They realize that if people are going to see the show, others will have to be backstage.
7. They are not afraid of death (it's not that dying doesn't bother them, but they fully understand Paul's words: "For to me, to live is Christ and to die is gain"—Philippians 1:21).[18]

Since that meeting of the Circle of Six, I've done some reconsidering. And I've discovered that my idea of old age is changing. I used to think that life was lived on a hillside. That you went up, up, up, until you reached about 50, at which point you hit an unavoidable banana peel and began a swift descent down the other side.

Paul's words make me wonder if I've had it backwards. As we grow older, the things that matter in heaven should matter more on earth. As we age, the stuff of earth should lose its value.

Rich people are those who know that the best is yet to come.

Rich people know that even if they've hit a banana peel, there's cheesecake ahead.

CHAPTER THIRTY-FIVE

The Last Laugh

*"I would not trade one moment of heaven for all
the joys and riches of the world, even if it lasted for
thousands and thousands of years."*

—Martin Luther (1483–1546)

SATURDAY NIGHT IS PIZZA NIGHT AT OUR HOUSE.
If you join us, you'll find yourself sampling some of the
finest pizza this side of Chicago. I should know. I made it.
In my opinion, if this pizza were sold on the open market,
it would cause the largest stampede since someone an-
nounced, "There's gold in them thar' hills." My wife
disagrees. She says this stuff would create the largest
stampede since my mother started passing out cod-liver-
oil pills. But that's okay. The kids seem to like it.

Sometimes during the eating of my excellent pizza, we
go to the living room and watch a video which has been
selected by the same method our forefathers used to select
videos: a democratic vote. Since my wife and I are out-
numbered, we have spent many years watching cartoons.
We have heard Bugs Bunny sing at the opera a hundred

times. We have watched Bambi's mother get shot repeatedly. We have seen Wile E. Coyote meet his maker on countless occasions right in our living room. Lately I find myself cheering for the coyote. But the ending is always the same. He never fails to fail. You'd think he'd learn.

Tonight I talked the troops into watching an old classic called *The Guns of Navarone*. It's a little heavy on the suspense, but I thought it would be just fine. Halfway through I realized my mistake. Halfway through I looked around me and saw children hiding everywhere, behind couches and chairs, holding pillows and blankets. And I wondered if we should revisit the Road Runner.

Pushing the "Pause" button, I said something that brought them out from behind their blockades. "Guys, you don't have to worry. I know the ending. The good guys lose."

"Dad . . . really?"

"I'm just kidding," I said. "But do you wanna know what happens?"

They wanted to know in the worst way. So I told them. The good guys win. It's as simple as that

"Now do you wanna watch it?"

They did. In fact, soon they were dropping pillows and creeping out of their shelters. Soon they were setting aside blankets and picking up the best pizza this side of Chicago. Even Ramona seemed to be enjoying it.

———

As a writer, I always look forward to opening my mail. But sometimes I wish I hadn't. Not long ago someone put my address at the top of a page and wrote these words below it:

Dear Mr. Callaway,

How can you write humor books when the world is falling apart? I think you need to get serious. . . . We are in the last days here and this is hardly a time for laughter.

I didn't quite know how to respond. In some respects the writer is right. We live in serious times. Like children sitting before the TV screen on a Saturday night, we're on pins and needles, wondering how a happy ending is possible. We read the papers. We watch the news. And we creep further and further behind our blockades.

Perhaps that's why I keep another letter handy. One I'll treasure for years to come. I've condensed it here for you:

Dear Mr. Callaway,

It's Tuesday today. Last Friday I visited my 85-year-old mother in the hospital. On my way to her room, I heard laughter. When I entered, I found Mom lying on the bed, surrounded by dozens of plastic tubes, a heart monitor, and a bedpan. She was reading one of your books and—despite her heart condition—laughing herself silly. Before I left, we spent some time talking about the hope we have as Christians and about heaven. Yesterday I received a phone call. Mom was with the Lord. It's been pretty tough, but I can't help thinking about the last time I saw Mom. I remember that she was laughing.

Sometimes I find myself pulling out that letter and reading it again. Sometimes I find myself thinking about an 85-year-old lady that I can't wait to meet one day.

I'm sure that lying on that hospital bed she wasn't thrilled with all that was going on around her. I'm sure, like me, she was concerned for her children. And her grand-children. But still she could laugh. Why?

Because she knew the ending.

She had read of things to come. Of a better place. A place where her tears would be wiped dry, her health restored, and her questions straightened into exclamation points. She knew that one day soon, she was heading Home.

———

Remember David? The kid in the wheelchair who hadn't a wish in the world? Well, before David died he did think of one wish. He asked his dad (a preacher) to preach at his funeral.

"Talk about heaven, Dad," he said.

And his dad did. Boy, did he ever.

For about 20 minutes he expounded brilliantly on the promise of the resurrection and the joys of eternity with Jesus. Then he did a most unusual thing. Stepping away from the pulpit, he walked down the platform steps and stood in front of David's open casket.

"David," he said, "we are far richer because you came into our lives, but now it's time to say good night. Good night, David. We love you." And with tears in his eyes, he gently closed the casket.

Then, turning to the audience, a beautiful smile stole across his face. "Good night . . . for now," he said. "But a good morning is on its way." With that, the song leader stood and started singing: "On that great gettin' up morning, we shall rise, we shall rise!" And the congregation joined him. Throughout the church, tears gave way to laughter and sadness to rejoicing. In the face of death, celebration had broken out. Death had been swallowed up in victory.

One day soon, those of us who have put our trust in Jesus Christ will take part in that victory dance. One day soon those arms that were spread wide on a Roman cross will open once again and welcome us Home to the richest life imaginable. A life that will never end.

Then why should we not live every day as though it were our last? Why should we not take God's hand and walk bravely into the future? I do not have a ready answer for the suffering and brokenness and pain that touch us all. But I do know in the very depths of my being that one day we will have the last laugh. That one day the tape will run out. The book will be closed. And all will be well.

Yes, life can be rich down here. But never forget, the richest life is still to come.

CHAPTER THIRTY-SIX

When I Hang Up My Sneakers

"Let us so live that when we come to die even the undertaker will be sorry."

—Mark Twain

Lately, in books and on the Internet, I've come across some humorous epitaphs. Believe me, there are some real winners out there.

In Enosburg, Vermont, an inscription over the grave of Anna Hopewill reads, "Here lies the body of beloved Anna, done to death by a fresh banana. It wasn't the fruit that laid her low, but the skin of the thing that made her go."

In Pembroke, Massachusetts, a weary homemaker lies below these words: "Everything here is exact to my wishes, because no one eats, there is no washing of dishes." A tombstone in Ruidoso, New Mexico, reads: "Here lies

John Yeast. Pardon me for not rising." An English lawyer by the name of John Strange had this pun etched on his headstone: "Here lies an honest lawyer, and that is Strange."

A woman in Key West, Florida, was married to a man who was known for his unfaithfulness. So she ordered a tombstone that read: "Frank, at least I know where you are sleeping tonight." So many tourists chipped away pieces of the headstone as souvenirs that she was forced to replace it without the biting commentary.

The grave marker of a couple from Prescott, Massachusetts, also reveals a great deal about their marriage: "Here lies the body of Obadiah Wilkinson and his wife, Ruth. Their warfare is accomplished."

How about you? What would you like on your tombstone? One lady answered, "I'd like it to say, 'See, I told you I was sick!'" Another said, "I'll just die if nobody comes to my funeral!" Let's face it, most of us would like to be remembered by someone. And what will they remember? I posed this question to some of the best-known Christians of our time. "What would you like to be remembered for?"

I think you'll enjoy their answers.

Josh McDowell, author and internationally renowned apologist, said, "Thirty years ago when God called me into the ministry He never called me to be successful. He called me to be obedient. And I'd like to be remembered as a man who was obedient and faithful right up to the end. I want to take as many people as I can with me to heaven, and enjoy life along the way."

Elisabeth Elliot, whose husband, Jim Elliot (famous for the words "He is no fool who gives what he cannot keep to gain what he cannot lose"), was killed by Auca Indians in South America, had a simple answer: "I want to be remembered as a servant of God. Nothing else."

Singer/songwriter Michael Card, best known for his song "El Shaddai," cowritten with John Thompson, responded this way: "My flesh says I want to be remembered as some great songwriter, but before every concert I've prayed, 'Lord, hide me in Yourself, don't let me be seen, let Christ be seen.' So I don't particularly care to be remembered. I would like my wife and kids to remember me as someone who loved them and cared more about them than myself. But beyond that I don't care to be remembered, because I've tried to point people to Christ."

Steve Green, another popular singer, recalled the words of R. A. Torrey: "You can't tell the effectiveness of a man's ministry until you see the lives of his grandchildren," then added, "After I am gone I pray that my children and grandchildren will be able to say that Steve Green was an example to them of faithfulness to God. That in spite of past wanderings my goal was to glorify Him."

Evangelist Luis Palau, who has spoken to hundreds of millions through his radio and television broadcasts, would like to be remembered "as someone who was faithful to Scripture. Someone who never ceased to preach the gospel of Jesus Christ to as many people as possible. That's what I love to do—faithfully present the gospel."

Following his brother's tragic death in a plane crash, author and psychologist Larry Crabb told me, "Since my brother's death, I'm realizing that I won't live forever. I hope that at my funeral, someone will be able to say, 'Here's a man who, more than anything else, wanted to know God'—that improving my golf game and selling books were not the things my life was organized around. My dad made a lot of mistakes—like any good father—but he gave me a sense that there is a dimension beyond what I can see. I remember as a five-year-old looking up at my father as he prayed publicly, and thinking, *He actually thinks he's talking to somebody.* I hope people will look at me and say, 'He really thinks there's somebody beyond himself.' "

Songwriter and singer Twila Paris, who wrote the popular hymn "He Is Exalted," said: "My father, my grandfather, and great-grandfather were ministers and I believe that many of the blessings I experience in my life and ministry are a result of the faithfulness of people I've never met. That makes me want to leave a legacy of faithfulness. After I'm gone, I hope that some young person who doesn't even know my name will be influenced towards the truth and the uncompromising position that Jesus called us to, because I was a thread and a link in the body of Christ. Because I was faithful."

Popular singer/songwriter Steven Curtis Chapman said: "I would like my wife to say, 'I saw his failures. I saw him blow it, but his greatest desire was to live a life that honored Jesus Christ.' I hope my children will say I was a committed father. And it would be nice if people remembered a song here and there, but that's pretty insignificant compared to my desire to know Christ and to make Him known."

One of the bestselling authors of our time, Max Lucado, told me, "I hope it will be said that I showed the splendor of God. That I showed why He is worthy of worship. That's what matters. Of course, I think I would feel like a failure if my children didn't remember me as a good father, too. That's what keeps me going." Then he added with a smile, "That and trying to break 90 on the golf course."

Author, speaker, and sociologist Tony Campolo said, "When I hang up my sneakers, I pray there will be hundreds of kids on the mission field because I helped them feel a passion for those who didn't know Jesus."

And popular songwriter Gloria Gaither, whose song "Because He Lives" has been translated into almost every known language on earth, summed it up this way: "If I had to write my epitaph, it would probably say, 'She gave herself away for the things that last forever.'"

And what would I like on my tombstone? Simply this:

> He found God's grace too amazing
> to keep to himself.

It won't make people laugh. Or be chipped away as a souvenir. But if it speaks of a life lived for God, graced by friendships, and nourished by joy and hope, then I will have lived the richest life of all.

Epilogue

A FUNNY THING HAPPENED ON THE WAY TO THIS conclusion. I struck it rich. Not rich by most people's standards, but certainly by ours. Unexpected book royalties and speaking engagements combined to finally coax our bank account into the black. We were shocked at first. Then we started looking around, wondering how we should spend it. Should we invest in growth income funds? In mutual funds? In stocks and bonds?

Or should we just blow it all at once on dinner at Taco Bell?

In all seriousness, the money amounted to more than we'd ever accumulated, and for the first time in our lives we wondered how to make our lives rich with a little extra money. I'm sure my parents would have paid a great deal to have this problem years ago. When they were first married, Dad asked Mom, "Would you like to open a joint savings account with me?" Mom said, "No, thanks, Honey. I'd rather open it with someone who has some money."

When Dad was my age he owned a life-insurance policy worth 25,000 dollars. But anything else was a luxury. The house was a rental. The car was a wreck. They had no investments. No savings account. No guarantees.

In fact, after I was born Dad cashed in the insurance policy to pay the bills.

As Mom and Dad moved into retirement, a secure future seemed out of the question. Their health was on the decline. Their expenses were on the rise. No longer able to look after a three-bedroom mobile home, they began walking through retirement homes asking lots of questions.

One day last spring, as my wife and I flipped through house plans, Ramona caught me a little off guard. "Why don't we put a suite in this house we're building?" she asked. "Your parents could live there."

A hundred mother-in-law jokes came to mind, but Ramona wasn't kidding. "They've been so good to us," she said. "If we can do it, I think we should."

"Would we put really good locks on the doors?" I asked with a grin. She said it was no problem. "Would we make it super soundproof?" She said we would. "How about an alarm system?" She said, "Now you're pushing it."

Over coffee and ice cream, we told Mom and Dad of our plans. Tears came to their eyes. But before long the tears were gone. Before long we had built them a custom-made suite with a view. A suite with their name on it. A suite they now call home. Sometimes we see them smiling like newlyweds. In fact, I don't think I've seen Dad this happy since the time he had his corns removed.

Often at night the kids disappear about bedtime. But we're not too worried. The other night I went looking for them, and there they were. Rachael was cuddled on the couch, studying the lines on Grandma's hand. Stephen lay quietly on the carpet, listening as Jeffrey read them all a bedtime Bible story. The story of Abraham, following God into an uncertain future.

I sat down on the couch, and thought of my parents' lives.

Many years ago Dad turned down a high-paying job to enter the ministry. I don't think he knew at the time how lean the years would be. I'm sure there were moments when he was tempted to regret his decision. Moments when he worried about his retirement plan. Would God really come through? Would the promise, "No good thing will He withhold from them that walk uprightly" come true in the end?

Dad knows the answer now.

After writing a long letter to thank us for his new retirement home, he told me, "Our dreams were never about good fortune. Instead, we dreamed of some years of faithfulness. And we got 55 of them. We dreamed of some kids who would love the Lord. And we got five of them."

I've traveled the world, but I've yet to meet two richer people.

A few months ago, each of us five children picked out something we would like to inherit when Mom and Dad leave this earth. I went with an object that sits upon their mantel: a small clock that chimes. It was a twenty-fifth anniversary gift 30 years ago, and it's as good as new.

When I was a boy I loved that clock. I loved opening the back of it. Winding it up. And watching it chime. That clock called me for breakfast and tortured me at bedtime. It crawled along during piano practice, and sped up on weekends. And I suppose, in some small way, it made me mindful that no matter what, time keeps ticking. That we should make the most of what's left.

One day this clock will sit on my own mantel, a reminder of the things that really count. A reminder of my parents' lives. Lives of faithfulness. Lives of service to God. Lives rich in texture and brimming with hope.

———•———

Like my parents' clock, may this book serve as a small reminder of the things that matter most. A reminder that the simple things in life are the best things. That friendship, peace, joy and hope are worth pursuing. And that they just may be closer than we think.

———•———

I'd love to hear from you. When you have a few minutes, drop me a note and tell me what has made your life rich. Until then, may God bless you. Richly.

> Phil Callaway
> P.O. Box 4576
> Three Hills, AB Canada
> T0M 2N0

Sources

Introduction
1. Cited in *Christianity Today*, "Inheritance Windfall May Bypass Churches," April 7, 1997, p. 58.

Chapter 1: Slowing Down in a Speeded-Up World
2. Tom Parker, in *One Day: The Things Americans Do in a Day* (Houghton Mifflin, 1993).
3. Dr. Kenneth Greenspan, director of the Center of Stress Related Disorders at New York's Presbyterian Hospital, reported by Rowland Croucher in *Stress and Burnout* (John Mark Ministries).

Chapter 3: A Parachute and a Promise
4. Charles E. Hummel, *Tyranny of the Urgent!* (InterVarsity Christian Fellowship, 1967), p. 5.

Chapter 5: Lifestyles of the Rich and Not-So-Famous
5. Due to the sensitive nature of some of the short stories throughout this book, the contributors will remain anonymous.

Chapter 8: I Beg Your Pardon
6. Quoted by Ron Mehl in *Surprise Endings* (Multnomah, 1993), p. 138.

Chapter 13: Your Own Backyard
7. Russell Herman Conwell (1843–1925) reportedly told this story over 6000 times. His lectures raised $6 million, which was used to found Temple University in Philadelphia, bringing to reality

his dream of building a university for poor but deserving youth who would otherwise be unable to afford college.

Chapter 19: The Power of Commitment

8. Quoted in *Discipleship Journal*, Issue 94, p. 16.
9. Quoted in *Calgary Herald*, April 9, 1997, p. D5.
10. Quoted in *Calgary Herald*, March 4, 1993, p. C2.
11. Dr. Paul Brand and Philip Yancey, *Pain: The Gift Nobody Wants* (Zondervan Publishers, 1993), p. 322.

Chapter 20: The Incredible Worth of a Memory

12. Reuters news agency report in *Los Angeles Times*, March 26, 1998.

Chapter 24: The Beggar and the Billionaire

13. Philip Yancey, *What's So Amazing About Grace?* (Zondervan, 1997).
14. Taped interview with Bob Van Kampen, July 15, 1997.

Chapter 25: Me and Jim Bakker

15. Taped interview with Jim Bakker, November 6, 1996.

Chapter 29: Walk with Me

16. Terry C. Muck, *Those Other Religions in Your Neighborhood* (Zondervan, 1992), pp. 150-51.

Chapter 30: Two Things Last Forever

17. C. S. Lewis, *Mere Christianity* (William Collins Sons & Co.), bk. I, p. 39

Chapter 34: Aging Grace

18. From a recorded interview in February of 1995. Gordon MacDonald expands on this in his excellent book *The Life God Blesses* (Thomas Nelson, 1995).

Make Your Life Richer Without Any Money

Phil is editor of *Servant* magazine, an award-winning publication read in 101 countries. A ministry of Prairie Bible Institute, one of Canada's largest Bible colleges, *Servant* is full of insightful interviews with well-known Christians, good humor, helpful articles, and world news. For a complimentary one-year subscription, please call 1-800-221-8532 or write:

Servant Magazine
Box 4000 Three Hills,
Alberta, Canada T0M 2N0

"With charming humor and gripping stories, Phil helps us take inventory of the things that matter most—both now and long after we've left this planet."

—TIM WILDMON, cohost of *Today's Issues*, and
vice president of the American Family Association

"This book is a winner. From its heartwarming stories to its crystal-clear message of simplicity, *Making Life Rich Without Any Money* will leave you challenged, changed, and chuckling. Don't just buy a copy of this book. Buy a dozen for your friends and family—and try to get a discount!"

—JOEL A. FREEMAN, author and chaplain of the
NBA Washington Wizards

"It is impossible to read this book without being changed. Changed in our demands. Our expectations. And our level of contentment. If you struggle to balance the stuff of earth with the demands of heaven, or if you long for a lightning bolt of joy, this is just the ticket."

—SIGMUND BROUWER, author of *Double Helix*

"In the middle of a very busy day, I began to skim this book. I was soon lost in laughter and wistful envy, then, encouraged that I can get off the treadmill of 'success' and start enjoying real wealth. If you have ever wished for a more simple, more fulfilling life, read this book."

—KEN DAVIS, motivational speaker and author

"Phil Callaway is absolutely incapable of writing a dull sentence. When he sets his pen to humor, the pages dance with laughter. When he undertakes a more serious topic the text shimmers with insight and wisdom—though humor is always around the corner! Here he offers fresh suggestions on finding the TRUE riches of life. Rewards that dwarf anything involving dollars, stocks, or bonds."

—PAUL L. MAIER, author of *Josephus* and
A Skeleton in God's Closet